SHIP TO SHORE

SWEET TO SHORE

CARIBBEAN CHARTER YACHT RECIPES

THE ULTIMATE IN DESSERTS

Author and Publisher ....Capt. Jan Robinson
Associate Publisher.......................Waverly H. Robinson
Associate Editor ....Barbara Lawrence
Illustrator/Cartoonist ....Raid Ahmad

If you are unable to obtain
SWEET TO SHORE
through your local store, write to:

SHIP TO SHORE, INC
10500 Mount Holly Road
Charlotte, North Carolina, 28214-9347

1-800-338-6072

For additional copies use order blanks in the back of
the book, or write directly to the above address.

First printing: September, 1990
Second printing: August, 1992

SWEET TO SHORE Copyright 1990

Printed in the United States of America

ISBN O-9612686-4-6

FOREWORD

From the beginning, man has been lured by those seductive sirens — the sea and romantic, far-away Ports-of-Call. As tremendous advances in sailing technology have broadened the range and increased the speed of sailing vessels, those once doomed to be only land-lubbers have flocked to the sea in unforeseen numbers. And with the greater focus of on-board creature comforts has come an ever-growing demand for fine dining at sea. The days when the sailor's meal was a salt-water biscuit and a piece of jerky are no more. The gourmet chefs have gone to sea!

No part of their task has challenged the charter yacht chef's culinary prowess more than the necessity and the desire to create a truly memorable finalé to a fine meal on board the yacht. Sea-going chefs have risen to this challenge with their customary creativity, ingenuity, imagination — and wit.

Desserts have been developed by design and discovered by accident. They have been created by smitten chefs and by politcally astute chefs - Charlotte Russe and Peach Melba come to mind. Thomas Jefferson sweetened *affairs of state* by serving às many as thirteen desserts at one meal, pioneered serving ice cream at state banquets and even introduced a concoction of pastry and ice cream later to become known as Baked Alaska.

Charter yacht chefs follow in the footsteps of their culinary forebears, reproducing and improving upon traditional desserts, adapting their preparation to the peculiarities of the yacht's galley and the availability of ingredients - and creating new desserts when circumstances demand. *Sweet to Shore* now brings you the best of the yacht chefs' desserts. You'll find preparation and cooking times, valuable hints, ideas for substitutions of ingredients, personal notes and the occasional bit of humor to help acquaint you with the creator of the dessert. So as you cap the perfect day on land or sea with a memorable dining experience, allow *Sweet to Shore* to provide you with the Grand Finale - the *Sweet*.

- Dr. Hal Hatfield

TABLE OF CONTENTS

DEDICATION

This book
is dedicated to the
Caribbean Charter Yacht Chefs
who by donating their most treasured
recipes made this book
a unique sweet
collection.

BREADS AND CAKES

NOTES

LOVER'S DELIGHT

Preparation time: 2 years
Cooking time: a lifetime
Serves: 2

Chef: Vanessa Owen
Yacht: Scarlet Rose

A wonderful husband
A red sailboat
2 dreams
Sprinkling of old friends
Pinch of ambition
2 sets of worried parents
Garnish: everlasting love

Take two very in love people and marry! Add desire to sail and red sailboat, combine dreams and ambition, encourage old friends to help realize the dream, reassure worried families and complete by sailing into the wild blue yonder. *Serve on calm seas and good winds.*

Best before initial ingredient is fully mature!

APPLE BREAD

Preparation time: 20 minutes
Cooking time: 50-60 minutes
Serves: 6

Chef: Wendy Smith
Yacht: Hiya

1 cup flour
1 cup whole wheat flour
1/2 cup bran cereal
1 tsp. baking soda
1 tsp. baking powder
1/4 tsp. salt
1/2 cup margarine
1 tsp. grated orange peel
2 eggs or substitute Egg Beaters
1-1/2 cups grated apples
2/3 cup walnuts, chopped

Preheat oven to 350 degrees F.
Combine the flours, baking powder, baking soda and salt.
In a large bowl cream together butter, sugar and orange
peel until fluffy. Beat in the eggs, one at a time, beating well
after each egg. Gently stir in flour mix, apples and walnuts,
just until combined. Spread into a greased and floured
8x4x2-1/2 inch pan or 4 small loaves and bake for 50-60
minutes. *Great for breakfast!*

Note: *This bread keeps well and freezes well.*

Make sure the oven is preheated to the required
temperature by the time the dough or batter is mixed. If
quick bread doughs have to wait, there could be loss of
the air that was mixed in and the bread will fail to rise
enough.

BANANA BREAD

Preparation time: 10 minutes
Cooking time: 70 minutes
Serves: 6

Chef: Kate Young
Yacht: Alize

1-3/4 cups flour
3 tsp. baking powder
1/4 tsp. baking soda
1/2 tsp. salt
1 cup mashed bananas
1/2 cup butter
2/3 cup sugar
2 eggs
1/2 cup nuts, chopped
1/2 cup raisins

Preheat oven to 350 degrees F.
Mix and sift first four ingredients. Beat bananas, butter, eggs and sugar until light and foamy. Add dry ingredients to banana mixture, stir in nuts and raisins. Pour into a greased loaf pan, bake 70 minutes and enjoy! *You don't even need butter with this one.*

BASIC MUFFIN MIX

Preparation time: 10 minutes
Cooking time: 15 minutes
Serves: 6-9

Chef: John Freeman
Yacht: Solid Gold, Too

1-3/4 cup flour
1/4 cup sugar
2 tsp. baking powder
1/4 tsp. salt
1 large egg, well beaten
3/4 cup milk
1/3 cup oil
1/2 tsp. dried orange peel
1/4 tsp. cinnamon

Preheat oven to 375-400 degrees F.

Sift together flour, sugar, baking powder and salt. Mix together rest of ingredients and add to dry mixture, blend together. Spoon into muffin tins and bake for approximately 15 minutes.

When working with baking powder or baking soda, do not beat the batter; stir only enough to mix it. Overmixing tends to make large holes in the bread and sometimes toughens it.

PUMPKIN BREAD

Preparation time: 30 minutes
Cooking time: 60 minutes
Serves: 8

Chef: Wendy Smith
Yacht: Hiya

1/2 cup margarine
1-1/2 cups sugar
1-2/3 cups flour
1/2 cup water
2 eggs
1 cup solid pumpkin (Libby's)
3/4 tsp. salt
1/2 tsp. nutmeg
1/2 tsp. cloves
1/2 tsp. baking powder
1 tsp. baking soda
1-1/2 tsp. cinnamon

Preheat oven to 350 degrees F.
Cream together the margarine and sugar, add the eggs, water and pumpkin. Combine all dry ingredients and add them to the above mixture, stirring well. Pour into 2 regular or 5 small loaf pans and bake for 1 hour.

This bread is the best! Also freezes well.

BRITISH SCONES

Preparation time: 30 minutes
Cooking time: 15 minutes
Cooling time: 30 minutes
Makes: 12

Chef: Jan Robinson
Yacht: Vanity

2 cups flour
4 tsp baking powder
Pinch salt
3 ozs. butter
1/4 cup sugar
3/4 cup milk
**Garnish: butter, raspberry jam, or jam of your choice
   and whipped cream**

Preheat oven to 400 degrees F.
Sift flour, baking powder, and salt into a bowl. Cut the butter into dry ingredients until the mixture is like fine bread crumbs. Stir in the sugar. Mix in sufficient milk to form a soft dough. Roll out to about 3/4 inch thickness. Cut into circles using a scone cutter or a floured glass. Bake on an ungreased cookie sheet for 12-15 minutes. Remove from oven, wrap the scones in a clean cloth. *When cool or cold, spread with butter (optional), jam and top with whipped cream.*

Note: *Very nice with a spot of tea in the afternoon.*

Scones are often baked on an iron griddle heated on top of the stove (or a cast iron skillet). The correct heat is important: if surface is too hot, the outside crust becomes too brown, leaving center uncooked. Test correct heat-sprinkle a little flour on surface of griddle; it should turn light brown in 3 minutes.

AMARETTO MOUSSE CHEESECAKE

Preparation time: 30 minutes
Chilling time: 8 hours
Serves: 8-10

Chef: Aija Eglite
Yacht: Rhapsody

Crust:
    2 cups Oreo cookies or chocolate wafers, crushed
    1/2 cup butter, melted
    1/4 cup ground almonds
Filling:
    1 envelope unflavored gelatin
    1/2 cup cold water
    1 (8 oz.) pkg. cream cheese, softened
    2 cups (16 oz.) ricotta cheese
    1-1/4 cup sugar
    1 (5 oz.) can evaporated milk
    1-1/2 tsp. lemon juice
    1/3 cup Amaretto
    3/4 cup cream, whipped
Garnish: crushed almonds and
    fresh strawberry halves

Crust: Combine cookie crumbs, butter, and almonds. Press into the bottom and up the sides of a 9-inch springform pan. Chill in freezer.

Filling: In a small saucepan, sprinkle gelatin over water. Let stand 1 minute. Stir over low heat 3 minutes. Set aside. Beat together cream cheese and ricotta 5 minutes. Add sugar and milk. Beat at high speed 2 minutes. Beat in gelatin and Amaretto. Fold in whipped cream. Pour into crust and chill 8 hours or overnight.

Prior to serving, sprinkle with crushed almonds. Fresh strawberry halves placed around the base of the cake makes a nice presentation.

BAILEYS, GRAND MARNIER CHOCOLATE CHIP CHEESECAKE

Preparation time: 20 minutes
Cooking time: 1 hour 30 minutes
Serves: 8-10

Chef: Wendy Riel
Yacht: Apjac

Crust:
 Vegetable (no-stick) spray
 2 cups graham cracker crumbs
 1/4 cup sugar
 6 Tblsp. butter, melted
Filling:
 2-1/4 lbs. cream cheese, softened
 1-2/3 cups sugar
 5 eggs, room temperature
 1 cup Baileys Irish Cream liqueur
 1/4 cup Grand Marnier liqueur
 1 Tblsp. vanilla
 1 cup semi-sweet chocolate chips
Icing:
 1 cup cream cheese
 1/8 cup Baileys Irish Cream liqueur
 1/2 cup powdered sugar

Preheat oven to 325 degrees F.
Crust: Spray springform pan with vegetable non-stick spray. Mix crumbs, sugar, and butter, then press into pan. Bake five to ten minutes.
Filling: Mix all ingredients together, except chocolate chips, adding eggs one at a time. Sprinkle half of the chocolate chips over crust, add filling, then sprinkle the remainder of chocolate chips over the top. Bake for 1 hour and 20 minutes. Let cool.
Icing: Mix ingredients. Put the icing in a pastry bag and decorate top of cake.

I usually decorate around the base of the cheesecake with fresh flowers. It's really pretty and dresses up any table.

EASIEST CHEESECAKE

Preparation time: 20 minutes
Cooking time: none
Serves: 8

Chef: Penny Knowles
Yacht: Golden Skye

1 (8 oz.) pkg. vanilla cookies
2 oz. butter
2 (8 oz.) pkgs. cream cheese
2 (14 oz.) cans sweetened condensed milk
Juice of two lemons

Crumble cookies, add melted butter and press into base of a 9-inch springform pan. Soften cream cheese; add sweetened condensed milk and beat until smooth. Add lemon juice. Pour mixture into pan and refrigerate until serving.

Note:*The lemon juice sets the mixture, it requires no cooking or freezing and with imagination has limitless variations, see below.*

Variations: 1. Melt chocolate chips (mint or plain) and swirl into filling; use chocolate chip cookies for the base. **2.** Try adding orange liqueur to filling and grated orange rind to base. **3.** Use Tia Maria or a coffee flavor in filling with crushed walnuts and cookies in base; decorate with walnuts.

IRISH COFFEE CHEESECAKE

Preparation time: 15 minutes
Cooking time: 30-35 minutes
Chilling time: 30 minutes
Serves: 12

Chef: Fiona Dugdale
Yacht: Promenade

Crust: 1 pkg. oatmeal cookies (crushed)
 1 Tblsp. dark brown sugar
 1/4 cup butter
Filling: 24 oz. cream cheese (softened)
 1 cup dark brown sugar
 4 eggs
 5 tsp. instant coffee
 7 Tblsp. Irish whiskey
 2 Tblsp. Kahlua
 1/2 tsp. vanilla
Topping: 1 tsp. instant coffee
 1 tsp. sugar
 1-1/2 cups whipping cream
Garnish: chocolate coffee beans, chocolate chips
 or chocolate shavings

Preheat oven to 350 degrees F.
Crust: Grease a 9 inch springform pan. Blend crushed cookies and brown sugar, add butter and press into pan. Set pan on a cookie sheet and bake 10 minutes. Let cool. Reduce oven temperature to 300 degrees F.
Filling: Blend cream cheese and sugar. Add the eggs one at a time. Add coffee dissolved in whiskey, Kahlua and vanilla. Pour over crust and bake in 300 degree oven for 30-35 minutes or until set. Let cool and chill.
Topping: Dissolve coffee and sugar in 1 tablespoon of cream, add remaining cream and whip until thick. Spread over top of cheesecake. *Garnish with chocolate coffee beans, chocolate chips or chocolate shavings.*

PUMPKIN CHEESECAKE

Preparation time: 35 minutes
Cooking time: 1 hour 5 minutes
Chilling time: 3 hours
Serves: 8-10

Chef: Liz Thomas-Gibson
Yacht: Tranquility

Crust:
  1-1/4 cups graham cracker crumbs
  1/4 cup finely chopped walnuts
  1/4 tsp. cinnamon
  5 Tblsp. butter, melted
Filling:
  2 (8 oz.) pkgs. cream cheese, softened
  1 cup sour cream
  1 cup sugar
  1 (16 oz.) can pumpkin puree
  1/2 tsp. cinnamon
  1/4 tsp. ground cloves
  2 Tblsp. Grand Marnier liqueur
  4 eggs, lightly beaten
Garnish: Whipped cream and pecans

Crust: Preheat oven to 350 degrees F. Combine cracker crumbs, walnuts and cinnamon. Pour on melted butter and combine. Press into a 9-inch springform pan and partway up the sides.
Filling: With an electric mixer cream together cheese, sour cream and sugar. Add pumpkin, cinnamon, cloves, and liqueur, beat well. Add eggs until just blended. Pour filling into crust. Bake for 35 minutes, turn oven off and leave cheesecake in oven with door shut for 30 minutes more. Cool completely then refrigerate several hours to chill. *To serve: remove outside of pan and add whipped cream and place pecans on top.*

Note: *A great replacement for Thanksgiving pumpkin pie.*

APRICOT AND ALMOND CAKE

Preparation time: 20 minutes *Chef: Penny Knowles*
Cooking time: 35 minutes *Yacht: Golden Skye*
Serves: 6-8

1-1/4 cups self rising flour
6 Tblsp. butter
1/2 cup sugar
1 egg
2 tsp. almond essence
Apricot jam

Preheat oven to 350 degrees F. Rub butter into flour and add sugar. Beat together egg and almond essence, add to dry mixture and combine. Mix should be stiff. Grease a 7-inch round tin. Put half of the mix in tin to cover the base, spread with jam and cover with remaining mix. Bake 35 minutes. *Serve warm or cold.*

SIMPLY SHAMEFUL

Preparation time: 15 minutes *Chef: Jan Robinson*
Cooking time: 1 hour *Yacht: Vanity*
Serves: 8-10

Cake: 1 box butter recipe cake mix
4 eggs
1/2 cup oil
1 (11 oz.) can Mandarin oranges and juice
Icing: 1 (9 oz.) container Cool Whip
1 (16 oz.) can crushed pineapple plus juice
1 box instant vanilla pudding

Cake: Preheat oven to 350 degrees F. Mix eggs, one at a time into cake mix, add oil and oranges, mix well. Bake in a greased bundt pan or baking dish. Cool before icing.

Icing: Mix all ingredients together well and frost cake.

LAMINGTONS

Preparation time: 20 minutes   *Chef: Jan Robinson*
Cooking time: 10 minutes   *Yacht: Vanity*
Makes: 18

1 Angel Food Cake
Garnish: Chocolate Icing (recipe below), grated
   coconut and whipped cream

Cut cake into about 18 pieces, 1-1/2x2 inches. Coat pieces, one at a time, with **Chocolate Icing.** I use tongs and dip cake pieces in chocolate, pour the chocolate over, or just cover the cake pieces however best you can. Quite a messy job, but fun. Roll in or sprinkle with coconut. Place on wire rack to set. *Before serving, slice each one horizontally in half and fill with fresh whipped cream. Decadent and delicious!*

Chocolate Icing:
   1 cup powdered sugar
   1 Tblsp. cocoa
   1/4 cup milk
   1/4 tsp. vanilla

Put sugar, cocoa and milk into a saucepan. Heat slowly, stirring all the time, until sugar is dissolved. Bring rapidly to boil and boil 2 minutes, or until icing forms a thread when it is dripped from the spoon. Remove from the heat, and stir in the vanilla. If the icing gets too thick, add a little water, or return to the heat for a moment.

BIRD'S NEST CAKE

Preparation time: 15 minutes   *Chef: Joanne Zanusso*
Cooking time: 30 minutes   *Yacht: Serenity*
Serves: 8

Fresh or canned apples, pears, peaches, or plums
2 eggs
1 cup sugar
1 cup flour
1 tsp. baking powder
1/2 cup milk
2 Tblsp. butter
Dash cinnamon
1/2 tsp. vanilla
Garnish: 1 Tblsp. butter, 1/4 tsp. cinnamon
  and 1 Tblsp. sugar

Preheat oven to 350 degrees F.
Grease an 8 or 9-inch round cake tin. Cut fruit into slices
and place in a circular design on bottom of pan. In a bowl,
beat eggs and sugar. Sift in flour and baking powder and
stir. In medium saucepan bring milk and butter to a boil
and add all at once to batter mixture and stir. Add
cinnamon and vanilla. Mix together well and pour over
fruit. Bake 25-30 minutes or until top is golden. Remove
from oven and let cool 5 minutes. Invert onto plate. Mix
butter, cinnamon and sugar together and spread lightly
over fruit while it is still warm. *This is a great morning treat!*
It's not too sweet.

Look honey, that one's just perfect for us!

MISSISSIPPI MUD

Preparation time: 10 minutes   *Chef: Sharon Davis*
Cooking time: 35 minutes   *Yacht: Que Sera*
Serves: 8-10

Cake:
   1 cup butter
   1/2 cup cocoa
   2 cups sugar
   4 eggs, slightly beaten
   1-1/2 cups self-rising flour
   1-2 cups chopped nuts
   Miniature marshmallows
Icing:
   1 box powdered sugar
   1/2 cup cocoa
   4 oz. butter
   1/2 cup milk
   1 tsp. vanilla

Preheat oven to 325 degrees F.
Cake: Melt butter and cocoa. Add sugar and eggs. Add flour and nuts. Mix together. Pour into a 9x13x2-inch greased pan and bake for 25-35 minutes.

Icing: Mix all ingredients until smooth. While cake is still hot, cover top with marshmallows. Put icing on top of marshmallows.

This cake can be divided and frozen for later use.

Carol Borden of Yacht Aquarius *adds 1 teaspoon vanilla and a pinch of salt to her cake mix.*

DELICIOUS APPLE CAKE

Preparation time: 20 minutes   *Chef: Kate Chivas*
Cooking time: 60 minutes   *Yacht: Tri World*
Serves: 8-12

**4 cups apples (peeled, cored and
  cut into small pieces)**
2 eggs, lightly beaten
1-1/2 cups sugar
1/2 cup oil
1 tsp. cinnamon
1 tsp. vanilla
2 cups flour
3/4 tsp. salt
1-1/2 tsp. baking soda
**Garnish: whipped cream, powdered sugar,
  or ice cream**

Preheat oven to 325 degrees F.
Put apples in mixing bowl and pour beaten eggs over apples. Add sugar, oil, cinnamon and vanilla. Stir well. Sift flour, salt, and baking soda, add to apples and stir. Bake in a greased 9x13-inch pan for 50-60 minutes.

Serve topped with whipped cream, powdered sugar, ice cream or plain.

If a cake breaks when turned out of pan, cut into cubes and serve with fresh fruit and a custard.

ONE-BOWL APPLE CAKE WITH CREAM CHEESE FROSTING

Preparation time: 15 minutes
Cooking time: 1 hour
Cooling time: 1 hour
Serves: 10-20

Chef: Jan Robinson
Yacht: Vanity

Cake:
   1 (16 oz.) can apple pie filling
   2 cups all-purpose flour
   2 cups sugar
   1/2 cup vegetable oil
   2 eggs
   2 tsp. cinnamon
   2 tsp. baking soda
   1 tsp. salt
Frosting:
   1 cup powdered sugar
   1 (3 oz.) pkg. cream cheese, softened
   1/4 cup butter, softened
   1 tsp. vanilla

Preheat oven to 350 degrees F.
Cake: Butter a 9x13-inch baking dish. Combine all ingredients in large bowl and blend well. Turn into the prepared dish and bake until cake tests done, about 1 hour. Cool.

Frosting: Combine frosting ingredients and mix to spreading consistency. Frost cake.

PIG-PICKIN' DELIGHT WITH PINEAPPLE PUDDING FROSTING

Preparation time: 20 minutes
Cooking time: 25 minutes
Chilling time: 20 minutes
Serves: 8-12

Chef: Kate Chivas
Yacht: Tri World

Cake:
   1 box Duncan Hines Golden Cake with Butter Mix
      (ignore directions on package)
   4 eggs
   1 (11 oz.) can Mandarin oranges
   1/2 cup oil
   1/4 lb. margarine, melted

Preheat oven to 350 degrees F.
Mix all the above ingredients with an electric mixer (medium speed) until well blended. Grease and flour two 9-inch round cake pans. Pour cake mixture into pans and bake for 20-30 minutes. Let cool, turn out of pans and frost.

Pineapple Pudding Frosting:
   1 (3 oz.) pkg. vanilla instant pudding
   1 large can crushed pineapple with juice

Blend both ingredients together well, spread on cooled cake layers and stack together. Refrigerate for about 20 minutes or until serving time.

Note: *You may prefer to delete part of the pineapple juice.*

A great cake for birthdays or any other special occasion.

PEAR CAKE

Preparation time: 7 minutes   *Chef: Silvia Schiltz*
Cooking time: 45 minutes   *Yacht: KEA 1*
Serves: 8

4 large eggs, or 5 small
3/4 cup sugar
3/4 cup flour
2 tsp. baking powder
1 Tblsp. milk
1/4 tsp. vanilla extract
1/2 cup butter, melted
4 fresh pears (peeled, cored and sliced into small
   pieces) or 1 large can
Garnish: powdered sugar

Preheat oven to 375 degrees F. Butter and flour a 9-inch baking pan. Beat eggs for 1 minute. Mix together sugar, flour, yeast, milk and vanilla. Add the melted butter. Pour mixture into a greased baking pan and add the pears. Cook for 45 to 50 minutes or until cake tester comes out clean. Remove cake from pan and sprinkle powdered sugar on top. *Can be served at room temperature.*

Hint: *Use a heart-shaped pan if you have one for a romantic occasion. Can be kept in refrigerator for 3 or 4 days, it gets better with time. This is also good as a breakfast dessert.*

Note: *I usually use 1 pkg. of chemical yeast, dry, but the "chemical yeast" Levure Chimigne can only be found in France or St. Martin. It does not correspond with the normal yeast, which has to rise normally so baking powder is a good substitute.*

MANDARIN ORANGE CARROT CAKE WITH ORANGE WALNUT FROSTING

Preparation time: 15 minutes
Cooking time: 45 minutes
Serves: 10

Chef: Nancy May
Yacht: Tri My Way

Cake:
   1-1/2 cups unbleached flour
   1-1/2 cups whole wheat pastry flour
   2-1/2 tsp. baking soda
   2-1/2 tsp. cinnamon
   1 tsp. salt
   1 cup grated coconut
   2 cups grated carrots
   1-1/4 cups sunflower oil
   2 tsp. vanilla extract
   1-1/2 cups honey
   3 eggs, slightly beaten
   1 (11 oz.) can Mandarin oranges, drained, chopped
Garnish: 2 tsp. grated orange peel

Preheat oven to 350 degrees F.
In a large bowl mix dry ingredients. Combine wet ingredients in a separate bowl. Pour wet into dry and mix well. Grease a 9x13-inch pan and pour in mixture. Bake 40-45 minutes until done. Cool, frost and garnish.

Orange Walnut Frosting:
   1 cup cream cheese, softened
   2 Tblsp. butter, melted
   1 tsp. grated orange peel
   6 Tblsp. honey
   1 cup walnuts, chopped

Blend first 4 ingredients until smooth. Stir in walnuts.

PENNY'S CARROT CAKE

Preparation time: 10 minutes
Cooking time: 45 minutes
Serves: 8-10

Chef: Candice Carson
Yacht: Freight Train II

Cake:
   1-1/2 cups oil
   1 cup sugar
   3 eggs
   1 (8 oz.) can crushed pineapple
   2 cups grated carrots
   1/2 cup raisins
   1/2 cup chopped nuts
   2 tsp. vanilla
   2-1/2 cups flour
   3 tsp. cinnamon
   2 tsp. baking soda

Icing:
   1 (8 oz.) pkg. cream cheese
   1/4 cup (2 oz.) butter or margarine
   1 cup powdered sugar
   1 tsp. vanilla
   1 Tblsp. milk

Preheat oven to 350 degrees F.

Cake: Mix oil and sugar. Add eggs. Fold in pineapple, carrots, nuts, raisins and vanilla. Sift together flour, cinnamon and baking soda. Add to first mixture. Beat well. Bake in a greased 9x13 inch pan for 45 minutes. Cool before icing.

Icing: Mix all ingredients well. Spread on cooled cake.

This is an adaptation of my sister, Penny O'Keefe's dough carrot cake.

CARIBBEAN POUND CAKE

Preparation time: 15 minutes
Cooking time: 35 minutes
Serves: 4-10

Chef: John Freeman
Yacht: Solid Gold, Too

4 large eggs
1 tsp. vanilla essence
1 cup margarine or butter
1 cup sugar
2 cups all-purpose flour
1 tsp. baking powder
1/4 tsp. salt
1/4 tsp. nutmeg
1/4 tsp. cinnamon
1/4 tsp. ground ginger
1/4 cup raisins
1/4 cup shredded coconut
1/4 cup cream of coconut (Coco Lopez)
3 Tblsp. honey, warmed

Preheat oven to 375 degrees F.
Beat together eggs and vanilla essence, set aside. Cream together margarine and sugar until light and fluffy. Gradually beat egg mixture into margarine mixture. Sift together flour, baking powder, salt, nutmeg, cinnamon and ginger. Fold sifted ingredients into egg mixture. Add raisins, coconut and cream of coconut. Mix well. Pour into a lined or floured loaf pan. Pour warm honey down the center of the batter and let stand 2 minutes. Bake for 35 minutes.

For a sweeter cake, line bottom of pan with pineapple rings.

COOL QUIK LIQUEUR CAKE

Preparation time: 20 minutes
Chilling time: 2 hours
Serves: 6-10

Chef: Jan Robinson
Yacht: Vanity

Cake:
  1 lb. Pound cake
Filling:
  8 oz. cream cheese, room temperature
  1/4 cup sugar
  2 Tblsp. Grand Marnier, Kahlua, or Triple Sec
  2 Tblsp. candied fruit, chopped (optional)
  1-1/2 oz. chocolate morsels
Topping:
  1 small (4-1/2 oz) Cool Whip
  2 Tblsp. Nestle's Quik or 2 tsp. cocoa

Cake: Slice the pound cake horizontally in 3/4 inch slices.

Filling: Beat cream cheese, sugar and liqueur, fold in fruit and chocolate. Spread filling between the layers and refrigerate at least 2 hours.

Topping: Beat Cool Whip and cocoa together and chill until frosting time.

FRESH LEMON CAKE

Preparation time: 20 minutes
Cooking time: 1 to 1-1/4 hours
Cooling time: 30 minutes
Serves: 6-10

Chef: Jan Robinson
Yacht: Vanity

Cake:
    1 cup (2 sticks) butter
    3 cups sugar
    5 eggs
    3 cups flour
    1/2 tsp. soda
    1 cup buttermilk
    Rind of two lemons
    3 Tblsp. lemon juice
Glaze:
    1/4 cup lemon juice plus 1 Tblsp.
    1 Tblsp. water
    1/2 cup sugar

Preheat oven to 325 degrees F.
Cake: Cream butter and sugar until light and fluffy. Add the eggs one at a time, beating well after each. Combine the flour and soda, add to the egg mixture, alternately with the buttermilk. Stir in the lemon rind and juice. Pour batter into a greased and floured tube pan, bake for an hour or until a tester inserted in center comes out clean. Glaze while still warm and in the pan, then let cake cool before removing it from the pan.

Glaze: Combine ingredients in a small saucepan. Over low heat, stir until sugar dissolves.

A special friend gave me this recipe - thanks Mildred!

RASPBERRY POUNDS ROYALE

Preparation time: 30 minutes   *Chef: Beth Avore*
Chilling time: 30 minutes or more *Yacht: Perfection*
Serves: 6-8

1 Sara Lee pound cake
1 jar raspberry jam
Garnish: fresh raspberries or frozen puree, Cool Whip

Remove cake from pan. Slice lengthwise 3-4 times to create layers. Use plastic wrap as base, lay bottom of cake down and spread with generous portion of jam, add next layer of cake, spread with jam. Repeat until you put the top layer of cake on. Do **not** put jam on top. Wrap and refrigerate until serving.

To serve: remove from plastic wrap, place on serving platter, slice 1/2-3/4 inch thick and put on dessert dish. Add cool whip and raspberries on the side.

Hint: *You can also use raspberry chocolate sauce for real decadence.*

Note: *This is a good first night dessert, easy. Plus, it lets you see how much the guests eat for dessert, by how sweet they create it, using what you serve on the side. Left overs are an excellent lunch dessert without the frills. For some, it is a great breakfast treat.*

STRAWBERRY CAKE SILVER SPIRIT

Preparation time: 30 minutes   *Chef: Emily Imbrogno*
Chilling time: 2 hours   *Yacht: Silver Spirit*
Serves: 8

3 (10 oz.) pkgs. frozen strawberries, thawed
2 Tblsp. Grand Marnier
2 Tblsp. fresh lemon juice
1/2 cup heavy cream
1 frozen pound cake
Garnish: Mint leaves

Puree 1 package of strawberries in blender, add Grand Marnier and chill. Drain the other two packages of strawberries in a colander over a small bowl. You should get about 1 cup of juice. Reserve strawberries. In small saucepan, bring juice to boil over medium heat and reduce by one-half. Cool slightly. Stir in lemon juice. Whip cream until stiff. Fold in reserved strawberries.

Cut pound cake lengthwise into 3 equal layers. Brush each layer with reserved juice. Spread 1/3 of the whipped cream mixture over bottom layer. Put second layer of cake on top and spread with 1/3 of the whipped cream. Put final layer of cake on top and spread with remaining cream. Cover and chill 2 hours.

To serve: cut cake into eight slices. Pour sauce (about 2-3 tablespoons) on dessert plates, lay slice of cake in sauce. Garnish with mint leaves.

CHRISTMAS COFFEE CAKE

Preparation time: 15 minutes   *Chef: Jolyne Grondin*
Cooking time: 30 minutes   *Yacht: Stowaway*
Serves: 6

Syrup and garnish:
   1/3 cup butter
   1/3 cup brown sugar
   18-20 pecan halves
   12-14 cherry halves
Cake:
   1/4 cup butter
   1 cup brown sugar
   1 tsp. vanilla
   2 eggs
   1 cup sour cream
   1-1/2 cups flour
   1-1/2 tsp. baking powder
   1 tsp. baking soda

Preheat oven to 350 degrees F.
Syrup: Melt in a saucepan the butter and brown sugar, stir. Place mixture in the bottom of a greased 10-inch tube or bundt pan. Decorate the bottom of the pan with the cherry and pecan halves.

Cake: Cream together butter and brown sugar. Add vanilla and eggs. Beat until fluffy. Blend in sour cream. Sift together flour, baking powder and baking soda. Make a well in the center of the sifted ingredients, add the creamy mixture, and stir gently. Pour into pan and bake for 30 minutes.

Note: *To decorate the bottom -- in front of each pecan half, put a cherry half -- makes a nice looking cake!*

COCKPIT COFFEE CAKE

Preparation time: 25 minutes   *Chef: Lindsay Geelhood*
Cooking time: 45 minutes   *Yacht: Voila*
Serves: 10-12

Cake:
   1/4 lb. butter
   1 cup sugar
   2 eggs
   1 cup sour cream
   1 tsp. baking soda
   1-1/2 cup flour
   1-1/2 tsp. baking powder
   1 tsp. vanilla
Topping:
   1/4 cup sugar
   2 Tblsp. chopped nuts (optional)
   1 Tblsp. cinnamon

Preheat oven to 350 degrees F.
Cake: Combine butter and sugar using an electric mixer. Add eggs and mix until smooth. Mix sour cream and baking soda together and add to mixture. Blend well. Add flour and baking powder, mix well. Blend in vanilla. Pour half of the batter into a greased 9-inch tube pan or angel food cake pan.

Topping: Mix together the sugar, nuts and cinnamon, sprinkle half of it over the batter. Pour rest of batter into pan and sprinkle the remaining topping mixture over it. Bake for 45 minutes.

This sweet treat also tastes great with your morning coffee in the cockpit. Add cold cereal and fresh fruit and you have a complete and nutritious breakfast.

FANTASTIC SPONGE CAKE

Preparation time: 20 minutes
Cooking time: 20 minutes
Serves: 6-8

Chef: Jan Robinson
Yacht: Vanity

Sponge:
   3 eggs
   1/2 cup sugar
   3/4 cup flour
   3/4 tsp. baking powder
   Pinch salt
   2 Tblsp. hot water
Filling:
   Your favorite preserves, or jam
   1 cup whipping cream
   Powdered sugar, to taste

Preheat oven to 375 degrees F.

Sponge: Grease and line two 7-inch springform pans. Place eggs and sugar in a deep bowl and beat until mixture is thick and will hold its own shape. Sift flour, baking powder, and salt together. Pour the hot water down the side of the bowl. Fold in sifted ingredients, about half at a time. Pour into prepared pans. Bake for 15 to 20 minutes, or until the sponge springs back when touched lightly. Cool for a few minutes in the pans, then remove to a wire rack to complete cooling.

Filling: Whip cream. Spread preserves or jam over one layer of the sponge cake. Pile whipped cream on top of the jam and spread it out to the edges. Carefully position the second layer of cake on top of the whipped cream. *Sift or dust powdered sugar on top.*

ISLAND SPICE CAKE

Preparation time: 20 minutes   *Chef: Jan Robinson*
Cooking time: 50 minutes   *Yacht: Vanity*
Cooling time: 10 minutes
Serves: 12-16

Vegetable non-stick spray
2-1/2 cups sifted cake flour
1-1/2 tsp. baking powder
1/2 tsp. ground cinnamon
1/4 tsp. *each* ground allspice, nutmeg and cloves
1/2 cup margarine, softened
2/3 cup brown sugar, firmly packed
3 egg whites
1 cup nonfat buttermilk
1 Tblsp. grated orange rind
1 tsp. vanilla extract
1 Tblsp. Grand Marnier

Preheat oven to 350 degrees F. Coat the bottom of a 9x5x3 inch loaf pan with cooking spray, then dust with flour and set aside.

In a large bowl combine cake flour, baking powder and spices, mix well. With an electric mixer, cream margarine; gradually add brown sugar, beating well at medium speed. Add egg whites, beat a few minutes or until well blended. Add flour mixture to creamed mixture alternately with buttermilk, beginning and ending with flour mixture. Mix after each additon until just blended. Stir in grated orange rind, vanilla and Grand Marnier. Pour batter into prepared pan and bake for 50 minutes, or until tester inserted in the center comes out clean. Cool in pan 10 minutes or so, remove from pan and cool completely on a wire rack.

Note: *This recipe appears to look time consuming, but it is easy, tastes great and only has about 140 calories per half inch slice.*

EASY RUM CAKE

Preparation time: 15 minutes   *Chef: Peyt Turner*
Cooking time: 60 minutes   *Yacht: Summertime*
Serves: 8 or more

Cake:
   4 eggs
   1/2 cup cold water
   1/2 cup oil
   1/2 cup dark rum (80 Proof)
   1 cap full Mexican vanilla (or 1Tblsp. vanilla)
   1 pkg. yellow cake mix
   1 pkg. instant vanilla pudding
   1-1/2 cup pecans or walnuts, chopped
Glaze:
   1/4 cup butter
   1/4 cup water
   1 cup sugar
   1/2 cup rum

Preheat oven to 325 degrees F.
Cake: Combine first 5 ingredients; add cake mix, pudding mix and half of the nuts. Grease a bundt pan, sprinkle remaining nuts on bottom and add cake batter. Bake for one hour.

Glaze: Melt butter, add sugar and water. Boil for 5 minutes, add rum *(don't sample too much while waiting on the cake!)* When cake is done, invert (or turn upside down) on cooling rack, prick holes, spoon glaze over top. Repeat until you have used all the glaze.

To serve: place on a cake stand, slice and eat. Yummy!

GREAT DRINK CAKE

Preparation time: 20 minutes　　　*Chef: Jan Robinson*
Cooking time: 1 hour　　　　　　　*Yacht: Vanity*
Cooling time: 1 hour
Serves: 8-10

Cake:
　1 box yellow make mix
　1 box instant vanilla pudding mix
　1/2 cup of oil
　4 eggs
　1/4 cup vodka
　1/4 cup Galliano
　3/4 cup orange juice
Glaze:
　1/2 cup (4 oz.) butter or margarine
　1 cup sugar
　1/4 cup orange juice
　1/4 Galliano

Preheat oven to 350 degrees F.
Cake: Mix cake and pudding mix together, add eggs one at a time, then mix in other ingredients. Beat well. Pour into buttered bundt pan and bake. Cool cake in the pan for about 30 minutes, then pour on half of the glaze. Let cool another 30 minutes, then loosen the cake and turn out on a cake dish and glaze the bottom side, now the top.

Glaze: Mix together all ingredients in a saucepan, bring to a boil and boil for 3 or 4 minutes.

Note: *The vodka, Galliano and orange juice is a very popular drink called " Harvey Wallbanger" - try not to test too much while making this cake!*

CHOCOLATE CHOCOLATE CHIP CAKE

Preparation time: 15 minutes
Cooking time: 40-60 minutes
Cooling time: 20 minutes
Serves: 8-12

Chef: Laura Flintoff
Yacht: Icebear

1 pkg. chocolate cake mix (pudding in the mix)
1 small box instant fudge pudding
2 eggs
1-1/3 cups milk
1 (12 oz.) pkg. chocolate chips
Cinnamon and powdered sugar
Garnish: mint leaves and chocolate syrup

Preheat oven to 350 degrees F.
Combine first four ingredients, then add the chocolate chips, mix well. Pour into a greased and floured bundt pan, bake for 40-60 minutes. Let cool, invert and sprinkle cinnamon and powdered sugar on top. *Garnish with mint leaves and chocolate syrup.*

Note: *This dessert is very, very rich, a definite chocolate lovers dream. To make this low in cholesteral substitute Egg Beaters for the eggs and skim milk for the milk. This recipe is a no fail one. I've added the ingredients in different orders and it always comes out perfect and gets rave reviews. It also works without using eggs, just turns out crunchier.*

When using cake mixes, put the water in bowl before putting in dry mix, then there won't be any dry pockets of powder on the bottom of the bowl after the cake is mixed. The powdered ingredients float on top of the water and mix evenly.

FUDGE TRUFFLE CAKE

Preparation time: 30 minutes　　*Chef: Liz Thomas-Gibson*
Cooking time: 35 minutes　　　*Yacht: Tranquility*
Chilling time: overnight
Serves: 8-10

1 (8 oz.) pkg. semi-sweet chocolate
1 cup sugar
1 cup unsalted butter
1/2 cup brewed coffee
4 eggs, beaten
1 cup heavy cream
1/4 cup powdered sugar
1/2 tsp. vanilla
Garnish: chocolate curls and fresh strawberries,
　cherries or raspberries

Preheat oven to 350 degrees F.
In a double boiler melt chocolate, sugar and butter. Cool.
Add coffee and eggs, beating well. Pour into a buttered and
foil-lined 8-1/2 inch springform pan. Bake for 30-40
minutes or until top forms a crust. Cool and chill overnight.
Cake may be frozen at this point.

*To serve: Whip cream with sugar and vanilla until soft
peaks form. Slice cake into pie-shaped wedges and top
with whipped cream. Garnish with chocolate curls and
fresh fruit.*

*You may also serve this cake whole, topped with whipped
cream, chocolate and fruit.*

MUCH BETTER THAN SEX CAKE

Preparation time: 15 minutes
Cooking time: 1 hour
Serves: 10 maybe

Chef: Jan Robinson
Yacht: Vanity

1 box chocolate cake mix
1 box chocolate instant pudding
1/2 cup oil
1/2 cup water
4 eggs
1 cup sour cream
1(12 oz.) pkg. chocolate morsels
1(6 oz.) pkg. butterscotch morsels
1/2 cup chopped pecans

Preheat oven to 350 degrees F. Mix in order given, add eggs one at a time. Fold in sour cream, morsels and nuts. Bake in a greased bundt pan, or a 9x13-inch baking dish.

Note: *I use a 9x13, as it is easier to cut into small pieces and take to the boat shows for samples!*

CHOCOLATE MACADAMIA TORTE

Preparation time: 10 minutes
Cooking time: 30 minutes
Serves: 6-8

Chef: Paulette Hadley
Yacht: Chardonnay

1 small pkg. chocolate pudding (not instant)
1 box devil's food cake
1 small pkg. chocolate chips
1 small jar macadamia nuts, roughly chopped

Preheat oven to 350 degrees F. Cook pudding according to package directions, remove from heat. Add cake mix, stir until blended, add chocolate chips and macadamia nuts. Bake for about 30 minutes (a spring form pan works well).

Hint: *A great back-up dessert, because all ingredients can be stored without refrigeration. Pineapple and cherries can also be added. Best if made a day ahead.*

CHOCOLATE TORTE

Preparation time: 30 minutes
Cooking time: 10-20 minutes
Chiliing time: 3 hours
Serves: 10-12

Chef: Jan Robinson
Yacht: Vanity

12 oz. semi-sweet chocolate morsels
1 (14 oz.) can condensed milk
1/2 cup butter
2 Tblsp. water
2 Tblsp. Kirsch
2 dozen lady fingers, split lengthwise
Garnish: 1 cup heavy cream, 1 tsp. vanilla,
    1 Tblsp. powdered sugar and chocolate shavings

In a double boiler, over hot water, combine chocolate, milk, butter and water, heat until smooth. Remove from heat and stir in Kirsch. Line 9x5x3 inch pan with foil, then line bottom and sides with 7 lady finger halves. Pour 1/3 of chocolate mixture over bottom layer. Use 7 lady finger halves to make next layer, cover again with chocolate. Repeat layers 2 more times ending with lady finger layer. Chill at least 3 hours. *When ready to serve, whip the cream with sugar and vanilla. Lift foil from pan, thinly slice the torte, place on individual dishes and dollop with whipped cream and chocolate shavings.*

Chocolate Lover...

GERMAN FRUIT TORTE

Preparation time: 20 minutes
Cooking time: 30 minutes
Serves: 6

Chef: Ronnie Hochman
Yacht: Illusion II

1/2 pkg. yellow cake mix
1/2 pkg. instant vanilla pudding
Fresh grapes, strawberries, kiwi fruit,
** Mandarin oranges or peach slices**
1/3 cup apricot jam
1 Tblsp. Triple Sec
2 Tblsp. water
Garnish: whipped cream

Make 1/2 package of cake mix and bake in flan or torte pan. Cool. Make 1/2 package of pudding and spread in indentation on top of cake, arrange fruit in artistic design. In saucepan, mix jam, Triple Sec and water. Heat until mixture turns into a syrup. Glaze torte with syrup. *Pipe whipped cream around edge.*

Instead of separating a cake or torte at the batter stage into two or three different cake pans to make layers, it's easier to use all the batter to bake one layer. Remove it from the pan after it has cooled and freeze in plastic wrap. When the cake is frozen, it is easy to handle. Slice it with a long, fine bread knife into as many layers as needed...they are flat and fit perfectly plus easier to frost.

NOTES

Notes

CANDIED ORANGE RINDS

Preparation time: 20 minutes
Cooking time: 20 minutes
Soaking time: 24 hours
Serves: 6

Chef: Anna Hancock
Yacht: Sly Mongoose

8 oranges
Water
2 cups sugar

Peel oranges and soak rinds in cold water for 24 hours or until white part is soft enough to scrape off. When all white is removed, cut rinds into thin strips. Boil them in water for 10 minutes and drain. Put rinds in sauce pan with the same amount of sugar (in weight) plus 2 tablespoons. Cook until rinds turn translucent. Spread on waxed paper to dry. *Great served any time, especially during Christmas holidays.*

Note: *Orange rinds will last a long time if kept in an airtight container.*

_ Gee, about time somebody left me something different beside milk and cookies!

CARAMELS

Preparation time: 10 minutes
Cooking time: 25 minutes
Cooling time: 30 minutes
Makes about 3/4 pound

Chef: Jan Robinson
Yacht: Vanity

6 Tblsp. sugar
1/2 cup pure maple or golden syrup
1/4 cup unsalted butter
5-1/2 ozs. half and half
1 tsp. vanilla

Generously butter 8-inch square pan and heavy 3-quart saucepan. Combine all ingredients except vanilla in saucepan. Place over medium heat and stir gently with wooden spoon until mixture is an even golden caramel color, very thick and breaks with big bubbles, about 20-25 minutes. (Test by dropping a little in cold water; it should form a firm ball.) Remove from heat and stir in vanilla. Pour into greased pan. Cool about 30 minutes, then chill. When ready to serve, cut into squares. Store in refrigerator.

CARIBBEAN ENERGY CANDY

Preparation time: 15 minutes　　*Chef: Jan Robinson*
Chilling time: 1 or 2 hours　　　*Yacht: Vanity*
Makes about 1 dozen

4 Tblsp. honey
4 Tblsp. wheat germ
4 Tblsp. crunchy peanut butter
4 Tblsp. shredded coconut
Garnish: 5 Tblsp. wheat germ

Mix honey, wheat germ, peanut butter and coconut together, refrigerate for 1 hour. Form into 1-inch balls, roll in wheat germ, refrigerate again. *A great high energy boost!*

CARIBBEAN BALLS

Preparation time: 20 minutes　　*Chef: Jan Robinson*
Cooking time: none　　　　　　*Yacht: Vanity*
Makes: 3 dozen

1/2 cup dates
1 cup dried figs
1 cup raisins
1/4 cup crystallized orange or lemon peel
1/4 cup crystallized ginger
1 to 2 Tblsp. lemon juice
3/4 cup walnuts, finely chopped

Mince dates, figs, raisins, peel and ginger in a food processor. Mix together well. Add lemon juice. Roll into small balls and coat in finely chopped walnuts.

CHOCOLATE ALMOND KRISPIES

Preparation time: 15 minutes
Chilling time: 30 minutes
Makes 3 to 4 dozen

Chef: Jan Robinson
Yacht: Vanity

1-1/2 lbs Hershey bars with almonds
1/2 cup chunky peanut butter
1 cup dry roasted peanuts
1-1/2 cups Rice Krispies
1 cup miniature marshmallows

Melt chocolate in microwave. Add peanut butter and mix until smooth. Combine cereal and nuts in a large bowl. Pour chocolate mixture over cereal mixture and mix. Add marshmallows and mix. Drop by teaspoonsful onto waxed paper lined cookie sheet. Put in refrigerator to cool.

COCONUT SUGAR CANDY

Preparation time: 10 minutes
Cooking time: 10 minutes
Serves: 10-20

Chef: Jan Robinson
Yacht: Vanity

2 cups grated coconut
2 cups sugar
1/2 cup water
Food coloring, optional

In a large saucepan, mix sugar and coconut together with water. Stir constantly over medium heat until mixture stops sticking to sides of pan and becomes thick; add a few drops of food coloring for an interesting appearance. Drop by teaspoonful on wax paper; let cool.

CREAMY PECAN PRALINES

Preparation time: 15 minutes
Cooking time: 10 minutes
Makes about 4 dozen

Chef: Jan Robinson
Yacht: Vanity

1 cup sugar
1 cup light or dark brown sugar
1 (5-1/2 oz.) can evaporated milk
2 cups pecan halves

In a saucepan over medium heat, combine sugar, milk and a few pecans. While mixture boils to a soft-ball stage, only stir around the sides. Remove from heat and stir in remaining pecans. Place waxed paper on a cookie sheet and drop mixture in teaspoonfuls. *Let cool, then eat - yummy!*

DATE LOAF CANDY

Preparation time: 10 minutes
Cooking time: 15-20 minutes
Serves: 6-8

Chef: Carol Cutler
Yacht: Got Lucky,Too

3 cups sugar
1 cup milk
1 (12 oz.) pkg. pitted dates, chopped
1-1/2 cups pecans, chopped

Put sugar and milk in deep pan and boil until mixture turns to a soft ball-like stage. Add dates and boil 3 minutes longer. Take off heat and beat until it begins to thicken. Add nuts. When very stiff, pour onto damp lint-free cloth and roll back and forth until you have a nice roll. Let dry, then remove from towel and wrap in foil. *This is a great recipe during the Christmas holidays.*

FANNY FARMER FUDGE

Preparation time: 20-30 minutes   *Chef: Liz Thomas-Gibson*
Cooking time: 10-15 minutes   *Yacht: Tranquility*
Chilling time: 1-2 hours
Serves: 8-10 or more

2 cups sugar
10 large marshmallows
1 (6 oz.) can evaporated milk
1 cup chopped walnuts
1 (6 oz.) pkg. chocolate chips
1/4 cup butter or margarine
1 tsp. vanilla

In heavy, large frying pan put the first 3 ingredients. Melt marshmallows and bring to a boil. Boil slowly, stirring for 6 minutes. In medium mixing bowl, put the remaining ingredients and pour hot mixture over and stir to combine. When cool, pour onto platter and chill to set.

GLEN'S KISSES

Preparation time: 2 minutes   *Chef: Suzan Salisbury*
Cooking time: none   *Yacht: Gypsy*
Serves: 6

1 box Perugina Bacci Chocolates
Garnish: a big, warm hug

Keep cool and serve liberally. A kiss is just a kiss until you taste the dark Italian chocolate bacci (kiss) which includes nuts and a kissing epigram.

PUSSER'S RUM TRUFFLES

Preparation time: 20 minutes *Chef: Penny Knowles*
Chilling time: 3 hours *Yacht: Golden Skye*
Makes about 16

4 oz. chocolate chips
10 oz. confectioners sugar
1 stick (4 oz.) butter
2 Tblsp. Pusser's rum
Garnish: cocoa powder or chocolate sprinkles to coat

Melt the chocolate, add the sugar, butter and rum. Beat until smooth. Chill for a few minutes to make it easier to handle. Form into small balls and roll in chocolate powder or chocolate bits to cover. Chill until hard.

These are delicious with after dinner coffee.

QUICK PARTY MINTS

Preparation time: 5 minutes *Chef: Jan Robinson*
Cooking time: 4 minutes (microwave) *Yacht: Vanity*
Chilling time: 30 minutes
Makes about 6 dozen

3 Tblsp. unsalted butter
3 Tblsp. milk
1 (15-oz.) box white creamy frosting mix
1 tsp. peppermint extract
Green food coloring

Combine butter and milk in 2-quart microwave safe measuring cup or bowl and cook on High until butter is melted, about 45-60 seconds. Blend in frosting mix. Continue cooking on High, whisking several times, until mixture is creamy, about 2 to 3 minutes. Whisk in extract and enough food coloring to give mixture light green hue. Drop by teaspoons onto waxed paper. *Let cool, then refrigerate until firm.*

THE ROYAL FUDGE

Preparation time: 5 minutes   *Chef: Jan Robinson*
Cooking time: 30 minutes   *Yacht: Vanity*
Chilling time: 30 minutes
Makes: 1-1/4 pounds

1/4 cup butter
2 cups sugar
4 Tblsp. water
1 (14 oz.) can sweetened condensed milk

In a large saucepan over medium-low heat; put sugar, butter and water, stir gently until sugar is dissolved. Add the condensed milk, bring to boil. Simmer on very low heat until mixture thickens and browns; stir occasionally. Remove from heat and beat well. Pour onto a greased cookie sheet. Cool until mixture sets, then cut into squares.

'SCOTCH - PECAN FUDGE

Preparation time: 5 minutes   *Chef: Jan Robinson*
Cooking time: 15 minutes   *Yacht: Vanity*
Cooling time: 1 hour or so
Makes about 30 pieces

1 pkg. butterscotch pudding
1/2 cup evaporated milk
1/2 cup brown sugar
1 cup sugar
1 Tblsp. butter
1 tsp. vanilla
1-1/2 cups chopped pecans

In a medium sized saucepan, combine butterscotch pudding and milk, add brown and white sugars, butter, vanilla and pecans; boil for 5 minutes, beating constantly. Remove from heat; continue beating until mixture holds its shape. Spread into a greased pan. Cool then cut into squares.

SESAME SEED BRITTLE

Preparation time: 10 minutes
Cooking time: 20 minutes
Makes: about 1/2 pound

Chef: Jan Robinson
Yacht: Vanity

3/4 cup sesame seed
1 cup sugar
1/2 tsp. vanilla

Preheat oven to 350 degrees F.
Spread sesame seed in large baking pan. Toast in oven for 15-20 minutes, or until lightly browned; stir occasionally. In heavy saucepan cook and stir sugar over low heat till melted and golden brown. Remove from heat; quickly stir in sesame seed and vanilla. Pour onto buttered baking sheet; spread thinly. *Cool and break into pieces.*

TANGY LIME CANDY

Preparation time: 5 minutes
Cooking time: 5-10 minutes
Makes about 32

Chef: Jan Robinson
Yacht: Vanity

1 cup sweetened applesauce
1 cup sugar
1 pkg. lime gelatin
Garnish: Sugar

In a small saucepan bring applesauce to a boil, stirring occasionally. Blend in sugar and gelatin, bring to a boil. Let cook gently for 2 minutes. Pour into a well buttered ice cube tray or a 9x4x2-1/2 inch loaf pan; chill until set. Cut into 1-inch cubes with sharp knife that has been dipped into hot water. *Roll cubes in sugar.*

TRUNK BAY DIVINITY

Preparation time: 15 minutes   *Chef: Jan Robinson*
Cooking time: 15 minutes   *Yacht: Vanity*
Cooling time: 1 hour
Makes about 40 pieces

2-1/2 cups sugar
1/2 cup light corn syrup
1/2 cup water
Pinch of salt
2 egg whites, stiffly beaten
1 tsp. vanilla extract
1 cup coarsely chopped nuts

In a heavy 2-quart saucepan combine sugar, syrup, water and salt; cook and stir until sugar dissolves, bringing to a full rolling boil. Slowly pour 1/3 of mixture over stiffly beaten egg whites, beating constantly. Continue boiling remaining syrup mixture until it will form a hard ball when dropped in cold water. Add remaining syrup gradually to egg mixture, beating constantly until cool and thickened. Add vanilla and nuts; beat until mixture holds its shape. Drop by spoonfuls onto waxed paper. Or, spread candy into a 10x6x2-inch baking dish and cut into squares. Cool thoroughly.

Cherry Divinity: Prepare as above, except fold in 1/2 cup chopped red candied cherries just before spooning mixture onto waxed paper.

VIRGIN BIRD NESTS

Preparation time: 15 minutes
Chilling time: 1 or 2 hours
Makes about 40 nests

Chef: Jan Robinson
Yacht: Vanity

1 (16 oz.) bag melting chocolate
2 -1/2 cups flaked coconut
1 cup small jelly beans

In top of a double boiler melt chocolate. When melted, stir in coconut until mixture holds its shape. Drop by tablespoonfuls onto waxed paper, forming circles. Make an indentation in the center of each circle; add 3 or 4 jelly beans. Allow to cool and harden.

Note: *Melting chocolate comes in a variety of colors.*

Hint: *At Easter, wrap the nests individually in cellophane to fill Easter baskets.*

VIRGIN ISLANDS FUDGE

Preparation time: 5 minutes
Cooking time: 15 minutes
Cooling time: 30 minutes
Makes about 2 dozen

Chef: Jan Robinson
Yacht: Vanity

2 cups sugar
1/2 cup crushed pineapple, drained
1/2 cup thin cream
1 Tblsp. butter
1/4 cup flaked coconut
1/2 cup chopped pecans

Mix all ingredients, except pecans. Cook to soft ball stage; cool. Beat until creamy, adding nuts. Pour into a buttered pan, cool and cut.

Hint: *Tint a very light green or red, if desired.*

Notes

COOKIES

Notes

CAPTAIN FOGGY BARS

Preparation time: 15 minutes　　*Chef: Nancy Drual*
Cooking time: 30 minutes　　*Yacht: Wind Gypsy*
Chilling time: 30 minutes
Serves: 6-8

1 tsp. vanilla
2 eggs
3/4 cup sugar
2 (8 oz.) pkgs. cream cheese
2 pkgs. frozen chocolate chip cookies

Preheat oven to 350 degrees F.
In a mixing bowl combine vanilla, eggs, sugar and cream cheese. Beat until all lumps are out and it is a smooth batter. Grease a 9x13-inch pan. Slice one package of chocolate cookies and place on bottom of pan. Pour in batter. Slice the other package of cookies and put on top. Cook for 30 minutes. Refrigerate. *Cut into squares and serve chilled...aways a big hit!*

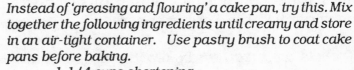

Instead of 'greasing and flouring' a cake pan, try this. Mix together the following ingredients until creamy and store in an air-tight container. Use pastry brush to coat cake pans before baking.
　　　1-1/4 cups shortening
　　　1/4 cup salad oil
　　　1/4 cup flour

BLUEBEARD'S TREASURE BARS

Preparation time: 20 minutes   *Chef: Ramona Polen*
Cooking time: 45 minutes   *Yacht: Empress*
Serves: 12

Batter:
  1/2 cup margarine, softened
  3/4 cup sugar
  2 eggs
  1/2 tsp. vanilla
  1-1/2 cups flour
  1 tsp. baking powder
  1/4 tsp. cinnamon
  2 cups fresh blueberries

Your Majesty... the treasure has been eaten!

Topping:
  1/2 cup flour
  1/3 cup light brown sugar
  1/8 tsp. nutmeg
  1/8 tsp. ground cinnamon
  1/4 cup margarine

Preheat oven to 350 degrees F.
Batter: In medium bowl, cream margarine and sugar, add eggs, beat well. Add vanilla. Sift together flour, baking powder and cinnamon. Add to creamed mixture. Spread batter into a buttered 9x13- inch baking pan, top with blueberries, then topping.

Topping: Mix dry ingredients in a small bowl, cut in margarine. Sprinkle over batter. Bake for 45 minutes, cool on wire rack, then cut into bars.

Travels well; can be baked the day before, cut into bars and wrapped individually.

GINGER SNAPS A LA TORTOLA

Preparation time: 30 minutes　　　*Chef: Vanessa Owen*
Cooking time: 10 minutes　　　*Yacht: Endless Summer II*
Makes 3 dozen

1-1/2 cups demerara or light brown sugar
1/4 cup molasses
1 egg, at room temperature
1 cup butter, melted and cooled
2-3/4 cups all-purpose flour
2 tsp. ground ginger
1-1/2 tsp. ground cloves
1-1/2 tsp. baking soda
1-1/2 tsp. cinnamon
3/8 tsp. salt
Sugar
Garnish: swirl of cream for each snap

In a large bowl, combine sugar, molasses and egg. Mix well, beat in butter. Stir in flour, ginger, cloves, baking soda, cinnamon and salt. Shape dough into 4 long logs, cut each in half cross ways, shape until diameter is 5/8-inch. Chill thoroughly.

Preheat oven to 350 degrees F.
Coat logs with sugar. Cut each log into 1/4- inch pieces and flatten to height of 1/8 inch onto a greased cookie sheet. Bake for 8 minutes until golden brown. Allow to cool slightly. Remove from tray (if they don't come off easily, reheat 30 seconds). Repeat until all dough is gone.

Can be stored for one month in an airtight container. Sounds complicated but once made, always made!

HANGTOWN BARS

Preparation time: 20 minutes   *Chef: Candice Carson*
Cooking time: 1 hour 10 minutes   *Yacht: Freight Train II*
Makes about 3 dozen

3/4 cup dried apricots
1-1/3 cups flour
1/4 cup sugar
1/2 cup butter
2 eggs, beaten
1/2 cup chopped nuts
1 cup brown sugar
1/2 tsp. baking powder
1/2 tsp. vanilla

Preheat oven to 325 degrees F.
In a saucepan, cover apricots with water, bring to a boil, simmer 10 minutes, drain, cool, chop (save for second layer of recipe). Sift one cup of flour with the sugar and cut the butter into mixture until it is like coarse meal. Pack into a 9x9-inch baking pan. Bake for 25 minutes. Combine eggs and brown sugar. Stir in 1/3 cup flour, baking powder, vanilla, nuts, and apricots. Spread over baked layer and bake 35 minutes more. Cool in the pan and cut into squares.

Note: *This recipe can be doubled and baked in a 9 x 13-inch pan.*

I got this recipe from my sister-in-law, Marty Carson, when she was living in California near a town called Placerville, formerly known as Hangtown.

MAMA'S LEMON BARS

Preparation time: 5 minutes   *Chef: Judy Garry*
Cooking time: 45 minutes   *Yacht: Sloopy*
Serves: 6

1 box lemon cake mix
1 stick (4 oz.) margarine or butter
1 egg
1 (8 oz.) pkg. cream cheese
1 box powdered sugar
1/2 cup chopped walnuts or pecans
Garnish: powdered sugar

Preheat oven to 350 degrees F.
In a mixing bowl, combine cake mix, margarine and egg.
Spread mixture in a 9x13-inch pan. Blend cream cheese
and powdered sugar. Spread on top of cake mixture and
sprinkle with nuts. Bake for 45 minutes. Cut into small
squares.

These make great snacks!

- *Personally I prefer having a dessert before
and after dinner!*

PEANUT BUTTER SQUARES
WITH CHOCOLATE

Preparation time: 20 minutes   *Chef: Laura Flintoff*
Cooking time: 8 minutes   *Yacht: Icebear*
Serves: 8-12

2 pkgs. graham crackers
1/2 cup butter
2 cups peanut butter
2 cups chocolate chips

Process crackers until very fine. Melt butter and peanut butter over medium heat until smooth. Add to the crackers and press into a 9x9-inch pan, let cool. Melt chocolate chips and pour on top, let cool and cut into squares.

Hint: Use a microwave to melt the chocolate chips: put them on high temperature for 2 minutes, then 1 minute more after the chips have melted. Try putting the mixture into paper liners, its quick and easy and has a nice effect. Also try mixing chocolate and vanilla or peanut butter chips together, this makes a nice marbled look on top. Another owner and crew favorite!

BLONDE BROWNIES

Preparation time: 10 minutes   *Chef: Peyt Turner*
Cooking time: 20-25 minutes   *Yacht: Summertime*
Serves: 8 or more

1 cup brown sugar
1/3 cup shortening, or butter
1 egg
Vanilla to taste
1 cup flour
1/2 tsp. baking powder
1/8 tsp. baking soda
Dash salt
1 cup walnuts, chopped
1 cup chocolate chips

Preheat oven to 350 degrees F.
In mixing bowl stir together sugar and shortening. Add egg, vanilla and dry ingredients. Add chocolate chips and nuts, mix well. Pour batter into a greased 9x9-inch baking pan. Bake for 20-25 minutes. Don't overbake, they should not get crispy.

Great as snacks, or after dinner. Serve warm, with ice cream. A smidge of Grand Marnier on ice cream is great. No complaints here!

– Honest guys, I'm from the Brownie family but they call me Blonde!

BUTTERSCOTCH BROWNIES

Preparation time: 15 minutes   *Chef: Suzanne R. Copley*
Cooking time: 20-25 minutes   *Yacht: Antiquity*
Serves: 10 or more

1/4 cup butter
1 cup brown sugar
1 egg
1 tsp. vanilla
1/2 cup all-purpose flour
1 tsp. baking powder
1/2 tsp. salt
1 cup walnuts, coarsely chopped*

Preheat oven to 350 degrees F.
Melt butter in saucepan. Stir brown sugar into butter until dissolved. Cool slightly, then beat in the egg and vanilla until creamy. Set aside. Sift together flour, baking powder, and salt into a mixing bowl. Slowly add to butter mixture. Mix well. Add chopped nuts (or nut/coconut mix) to butter mixture. Pour batter into greased 9x9-inch cake pan. Bake 20-25 minutes. Do **not** overbake. Brownies are a chewy, rich confection. Cut into bars when cool. *Enjoy!*

* For variety try 1/2 cup chopped walnuts and 1/2 cup grated coconut instead of the whole cup of walnuts.

When mixing anything using eggs and shortening, try dropping an egg in a measuring cup first. Make sure egg white coats all sides. Empty egg out, then measure the shortening and see how nicely it leaves the cup.

CAN'T RESIST "BROWNIES"

Preparation time: 15 minutes   *Chef: Joanne Zanusso*
Cooking time: 30 minutes   *Yacht: Serenity*
Serves: 8

1 cup butter
7 Tblsp. cocoa
2 cups sugar
4 eggs, beaten
1 tsp. vanilla or peppermint extract
1-1/2 cups flour
1 tsp. baking powder
1 cup nuts, chopped (optional)
Garnish: whole pecans, if desired

Preheat oven to 350 degrees F.
In saucepan melt butter, cocoa and sugar over medium heat. Stir until smooth. Add beaten eggs. Slowly stir in the rest of the ingredients. Pour into a lightly greased 8-inch square pan. Bake for no more than 30 minutes, cool and cut.

Note: *I use whole pecans to garnish before baking or if peppermint flavoring is used, garnish with chocolate-mint wafers. Very moist and chewy!*

CREAM CHEESE BROWNIES

Preparation time: 20 minutes
Cooking time: 40-45 minutes
Serves: 15

Chef: Vivian Phelps
Yacht: Encore

Brownies:
   1 box chocolate cake mix
   1 stick (4 oz.) margarine
   2 eggs
   2 tsp. vanilla
Topping:
   1 (8 oz.) pkg. cream cheese
   1 box confectioners' sugar
   2 eggs
   2 tsp. vanilla
Garnish: chopped pecans

Preheat oven to 350 degrees F.
Brownies: Mix ingredients together and put into a greased 9x13-inch pan.

Topping: Mix ingredients and spread on top of other mixture, sprinkle with chopped pecans. Bake for 40-45 minutes. Test with a toothpick for doneness. There should be a few crumbs.

BEST EVER CHOCOLATE CHIP COOKIES

Preparation time: 20 minutes
Cooking time: 10 minutes
Cooling time: 15 minutes
Serves: 1-12

Chef: Joanne Zanusso
Yacht: Serenity

1 cup butter*
2 cups brown sugar
2 cups flour
1 tsp. baking soda
2 tsp. vanilla
2 eggs
2 cups chocolate chips

***You may substitute 1/2 cup peanut butter for a 1/2 cup of butter...may need a little more flour in this case.**

Preheat oven to 300-325 degrees F.
In a large mixing bowl cream butter and sugar, beat in eggs and vanilla. Stir flour and baking soda together, add to butter and egg mixture. Stir in chocolate chips. Drop by spoonfuls onto a lightly greased cookie sheet. Bake 10 minutes. *Cool then eat! These freeze well.*

Hint: *The secret to chewy cookies is the low oven temperature and to remove them when they are pale brown. Cookies will continue to crisp while cooling.*

If you have trouble with drop cookies spreading, try this: after spooning chilled dough onto a cookie sheet, place the sheet in the refrigerator for ten to fifteen minutes before baking. This allows the spooned cookies to rechill.

CHOCOLATE CHIPS

Preparation time: 20 minutes   *Chef: Laura Flintoff*
Cooking time: 10 minutes   *Yacht: Icebear*
Makes about 3 dozen

1 cup butter (8 oz.) and 2 Tblsp. margarine
1-1/2 cups brown sugar
1 tsp. vanilla
2 eggs or 1/2 cup Egg Beaters
1 tsp. salt
1/2 tsp. cinnamon
1/4 tsp. baking soda
2-1/2 - 3 cups all-purpose flour
12 oz. or 2 cups chocolate chips
1 cup chopped pecans

Preheat oven to 375 degrees F.
Cream butter and margarine until soft and light yellow.
Add brown sugar and vanilla, cream until light and fluffy.
Add eggs one at a time, mix until incorporated. Mix dry
ingredients together and add slowly to butter mixture. Add
chocolate chips and nuts. Drop by tablespoonfuls onto
cookie sheet. Bake for 10 minutes. Let cool 1-2 minutes
before moving onto racks.

Hint: *Add 1-3 tablespoons of cocoa powder for more chocolate
flavor and dark color. This is the owner and crew's most
favorite cookie in the whole world!*

*When a cookie recipe directs you to 'drop from a spoon'
try a knife instead. Dip knife in glass of water, pass it
thru cookie dough in bowl, scoop it up and roll it off with
your finger. It works much easier and isn't as messy.*

THE BEST CHOCOLATE CHIP COOKIES

Preparation time: 10 minutes
Cooking time: 10-12 minutes
Makes: 24 cookies

Chef: Vivian Phelps
Yacht: Encore

2-1/4 cups super chunky peanut butter
2 cups oats
4 large eggs
1-1/2 cups sugar
1-1/2 cups brown sugar
1-1/2 tsp. baking soda
1 tsp. vanilla
12 oz. Hershey's chocolate chips

Preheat oven to 350 degrees F.
Blend all ingredients, adding chocolate chips last. Use a teaspoon to drop on a lightly greased cookie sheet. Bake for 10-12 minutes; remove from oven while soft and let stand on cookie sheet 5 minutes before removing.

sweet Dreams!

COCOA OAT BOAT COOKIES

Preparation time: 15 minutes
Cooking time: 3 minutes
Chilling time: 30 minutes
Makes about 3 dozen

Chef: Carole Borden
Yacht: Aquarius

2 cups sugar
1/2 cup milk
1/3 cup cocoa
1/2 cup margarine
1 tsp. vanilla
3 Tblsp. peanut butter
3 cups quick oats or regular oats
1/2 cup *each* chopped nuts and raisins (optional)

In a saucepan boil together sugar, milk, cocoa, and margarine for 3 minutes. Remove from heat, add peanut butter, stir until melted. Add vanilla, oats, nuts and raisins. Drop by the teaspoonful onto waxed paper and cool completely. *Great taste with ease.*

NORTH SWELL COOKIES

Preparation time: 15 minutes
Cooking time: 10 minutes
Makes 24

Chef: Suzan Salisbury
Yacht: Gypsy

1/4 cup vegetable oil
1 cup brown sugar
1 egg
1 cup all-purpose flour
1/4 tsp. salt
2 tsp. vanilla
1 cup broken nuts

Preheat oven to 350 degrees F.
Combine oil and sugar in a bowl, add egg and mix well. Stir in flour, salt, and vanilla, stir in the nuts. Drop by heaping teaspoonfuls onto cookie sheet and bake 8-10 minutes.

GREAT COOKIES

Preparation time: 30 minutes   *Chef: Jan Robinson*
Cooking time: 20 minutes   *Yacht: Vanity*
Makes about 40

Cookies:
  7 ozs. butter
  1/2 cup lightly backed brown sugar
  1-1/2 cups flour
  1/2 tsp. baking powder
  3 Tblsp. cocoa
  2 cups cornflakes
Icing:
  2 cups powdered sugar
  4 tsp. cocoa
  Water to mix
Garnish: walnut or pecan halves

Preheat oven to 350 degrees F.
Cookies: Cream the butter and sugar until soft and fluffy.
Sift the flour, baking powder and cocoa into creamed
mixture. Mix well. Add the cornflakes and mix thoroughly.
Put heaping teaspoonfuls of mixture on a greased cookie
sheet. Bake for 15-20 minutes. Allow to cool before icing.

Icing: Sift powdered sugar and cocoa together, add
sufficient water to form a stiff icing. *Top each cookie with
icing and a walnut or pecan half.*

BUTTER OATMEAL COOKIES

Preparation time: 15 minutes
Cooking time: 10 minutes
Makes 24-30

Chef: Connie Frey
Yacht: Jewell

1 cup margarine
1 cup powdered sugar
2 tsp. vanilla
1-1/4 cup flour
1/4 tsp. salt
1 cup dry oatmeal
Garnish: whole pecan or walnut meats

Preheat oven to 350 degrees F.
In a large mixing bowl combine margarine, powdered sugar and vanilla, beat well. Add remaining ingredients and mix well. Roll into small balls about the size of a walnut and press flat with a fork. If desired, place a whole pecan or walnut meat on top of cookie. *Bake 10-12 minutes.*

Note: *The kids will enjoy helping with this simple but yummy recipe.*

Recrisp cookies by baking in a 400 degrees F. oven for about 3 minutes.

ICED REFRIGERATOR BISCUITS

Preparation time: 30 minutes
Cooking time: 20 minutes
Chilling time: 30 minutes
Makes 30

Chef: Jan Robinson
Yacht: Vanity

Biscuits:
   7 ozs. butter
   3/4 cup brown sugar
   2 cups flour
   1/4 tsp. salt
Decoration:
   6 ozs. dark cooking chocolate
   1 tsp. Crisco
Garnish: finely chopped walnuts, or pecans
   and grated coconut

Biscuits: Cream butter and brown sugar together until light and fluffy. Sift the flour and salt, and gradually add to creamed mixture to form a firm dough. Place dough on a lightly floured board, and form into two, 4-inch long rolls. Wrap separately in greaseproof paper and allow to chill for at least 30 minutes until firm or overnight.

Preheat oven to 325 degrees F. Cut rolls into 3/4-inch slices, and place on greased oven trays. Bake for 15-20 minutes or until pale golden brown. Cool on wire rack.

Decoration: Melt chocolate and Crisco gently in the top of a double boiler. Remove from heat. Dip biscuits in chocolate to half coat them diagonally. Sprinkle them with chopped nuts and/or coconut.

Note: *When chocolate is set, biscuits may be stored in an airtight container, if they don't disappear first!*

MELTAWAYS

Preparation time: 5-10 minutes
Cooking time: 10-12 minutes
Makes: about 2 dozen

Chef: Nancy May
Yacht: Tri My Way

Dough:
   1 cup butter
   3/4 cup cornstarch
   1/2 cup powdered sugar
   1 cup unbleached flour
Glaze:
   3 oz. cream cheese
   1 tsp. vanilla
   1 cup powdered sugar

Preheat oven to 350 degrees F.
Dough: Combine butter, cornstarch, powdered sugar and flour. Beat together well. Drop teaspoonfuls on a cookie sheet, bake 10-12 minutes or until a very light golden color.

Glaze: Mix glaze ingredients together. Spoon a little on each cookie while still warm.

When baking cookies in large amounts, cut two pieces of foil the size of cookie sheet. Place unbaked cookies on each piece of foil; refrigerate, if possible. Place the foil and cookies on sheet and bake as usual. When finished, slide foil off and slide next foil with cookie dough on, again placing in oven. Cookie sheet is already hot, so cuts down baking time by 2 or 3 minutes.

MELTING MOMENTS

Preparation time: 35 minutes
Cooking time: 20 minutes
Makes 2 dozen

Chef: Jan Robinson
Yacht: Vanity

Cookie:
   7 ozs. butter
   1/2 cup powdered sugar
   1/2 tsp. vanilla essence
   1 cup flour
   1 cup corn flour
   1/2 tsp. salt
Filling:
   1-1/2 cups powdered sugar
   1/2 tsp. vanilla essence
   Water

Preheat oven to 325 degrees F.
Cookies: Cream butter and powdered sugar until very soft. Add vanilla essence. Sift flour, corn flour and salt into the creamed mixture and work until a smooth stiff dough is formed. Pull off pieces of the dough and roll into balls. Place on a greased cookie sheet and press with a fork to flatten, or pipe with a large star nozzle. Bake for about 20 minutes. Do not allow the cookies to get much color. When cooled, sandwich together with jam or filling.

Filling: Sift the powdered sugar, add the vanilla and sufficient water to form a stiff icing.

To avoid excessive browning, use solid vegetable shortening as opposed to butter or oil to grease baking sheets or foil.

SAND DOLLARS

Preparation time: 30 minutes
Cooking time: 20 minutes
Serves: 8-10

Chef: Lindsay Geelhood
Yacht: Voila

2 cups flour, sifted
3 heaping Tblsp. powdered sugar
1 cup butter, softened
1 Tblsp. water
1 tsp. vanilla
Garnish: 1/2 cup powdered sugar

Preheat oven to 325 degrees F.
Mix flour and powdered sugar together, add butter. Add water and vanilla, mixing well. Roll into small balls and place on cookie sheet. Press lightly on each ball with a spoon to flatten just a little. Bake about 20 minutes. Remove from oven and cool slightly. Roll each cookie in powdered sugar while still warm.

*We recommend that you use **real** butter and double this recipe so that you will have plenty on hand for the cookie monsters in your crew.*

Jumbo is my name
Bake is my Game...

CHIACCHERE

Preparation time: 20 minutes
Cooking time: 40 minutes
Serves: 10-15

Chef: Anna Hancock
Yacht: Sly Mongoose

2 cups flour
3 eggs
1/2 cup butter, softened
1-1/2 tsp. baking powder
2 tsp. vanilla
1/2 tsp. salt
Milk, as needed
Oil to fry
Garnish: powdered sugar

Place flour in a mixing bowl, add the next 5 ingredients one by one, stirring with a wooden spoon, then work mixture with your hands on a flat surface until you reach a stiff dough, add a little milk if needed. Roll dough to a 1/8-inch thickness. Cut dough into the shape you prefer, but no longer than 7-inches. Fry in very hot oil until golden in color, drain. *Sprinkle with powdered sugar.*

Very nice served at a party or on a buffet. Excellent when accompanied by champagne or a very dry white wine. **Chiacchere** *is an Italian snack, usually served at Carnival Time.*

Tip: *For best results cut dough with a crimper.*

FLY CEMETERY

Preparation time: 20 minutes
Cooking time: 20-25 minutes
Chilling time: 30 minutes
Serves: 6

Chef: Marilyn Stenberg
Yacht: Sabina D

8 oz. short crust pastry, or pie crust mix
1/2 cup currants
2 large pinches cinnamon
2 Tblsp. sugar
4 Tblsp. thick custard*
2 Tblsp. butter, cut into small pieces
Milk
Sugar
Garnish: additional custard or
whipped cream on side

***Ordinary packet variety can be used and should be fairly sticky in consistency.**

Preheat oven to 450 degrees F.
Divide the pastry in half and roll out one half on a lightly floured surface to fit a shallow greased 18x7-inch tin. Mix currants, cinnamon and sugar with enough custard to make a sticky mixture. Spread evenly on the pastry in the tin and dot with butter. Roll out the remaining pastry to same size. Put it on top and seal edges well. Use a fork to crimp the edges, lightly score the pastry and make a couple of steam holes. Brush with milk, sprinkle with sugar and bake for 20-25 minutes. Cool in the tin, then transfer to a wire tray. *Cut into squares and serve cold.*

Note: *This pastry will store in an airtight container for 4 days.*

MERINGUES

Preparation time: 20 minutes
Cooking time: 1-1/2 hours
Makes about 40

Chef: Jan Robinson
Yacht: Vanity

4 egg whites
1 cup superfine sugar
1/4 tsp. vanilla essence
Whipped cream

Preheat oven to 250 degrees F.
Have the egg whites at room temperature. Beat the egg whites lightly in a bowl. Add the sugar, a little at a time, beating well after each addition. Add vanilla and continue beating until meringue is stiff and glossy. Cover a cookie sheet with aluminium foil and grease. Place the mixture in heaping teaspoonfuls on the foil. Allow space for the meringues to expand. Bake for 1-1/2 to 2 hours, or until dry. Allow to cool.

To serve, join the meringues together with flavored whipped cream, or see **Frozen Liqueur Souffle** recipe on page 145.

Hint: *These are a great standby for a quick dessert. Before filling with cream, store in an airtight container, a party piece is always at hand.*

CHOCOLATE CRACKLES

Preparation time: 30 minutes
Chilling time: 4 hours
Cooking time: 15 minutes
Makes 4-6 dozen

Chef: Sheila Kruse Boyce
Yacht: Victorious

4 oz. unsweetened chocolate
1/2 cup salad oil
2 cups sugar
4 eggs
2 tsp. vanilla
2 cups all-purpose flour
2 tsp. baking powder
1/2 tsp. salt
1/2 cup nuts, chopped
1 cup powdered sugar
Optional: 1/4 cup Grand Marnier plus
**   3 Tblsp. flour, less 1 tsp. vanilla**

Preheat oven to 350 degrees F.
Melt chocolate in top of double boiler or microwave. Remove from heat, blend in oil, Grand Marnier (if desired) and sugar. Add eggs one at a time, beating well after each addition. Add vanilla. Sift together flour, baking powder and salt, stir into chocolate mixture. Add nuts. Chill soft dough several hours or overnight. Shape into small balls and roll in powdered sugar. Bake on a greased cookie sheet. *Check for doneness with a toothpick, they should be somewhat soft.*

These are the lightest, fudgiest, most amazing cookies I've ever tasted...and your guests will say the same! Judged 5th in the dessert category in 1989 VICL Grand Marnier cooking competition.

SCRUNCHY MACAROONS

Preparation time: 10 minutes   *Chef: Shirley Benjamin*
Cooking time: 25 minutes   *Yacht: Verano Sin Final*
Serves: 8

3 cups grated coconut
2/3 cup sugar
1/3 cup flour
1/4 tsp. salt
3 large egg whites
1 tsp. almond extract
1 cup flaked almonds
1/2 cup chopped green and red candied cherries

Preheat oven to 325 degrees F.
Mix together coconut, sugar, flour and salt. Stir in egg whites and almond extract. Add almonds and cherries. Drop by teaspoonfuls onto a baking sheet. Bake until edges are golden and remove at once from the baking sheet.

Tinted coconut: place shredded or flaked coconut in a screw-top jar; add a few drops of desired food coloring. Secure lid and shake till all is colored.

Notes

CREPES, FONDUES AND FRITTERS

Notes

BANANA CREPES

Preparation time: 30 minutes
Cooking time: 30 minutes
Serves: 6

Chef: Wendy Reil
Yacht: Apjac

Crepes:
- **1-1/2 cups flour**
- **1 Tblsp. sugar**
- **1/2 tsp. baking powder**
- **1/2 tsp. salt**
- **2 cups milk**
- **2 eggs**
- **2 Tblsp. butter (melted)**
- **1/2 tsp. vanilla**

Filling:
- **5 bananas, peeled and thinly sliced**
- **1/2 cup brown sugar**
- **1/2 cup raisins**
- **1/2 cup walnuts**
- **Rum (to taste)***
- **Amaretto (to taste)***
- **1/3 cup butter**

Garnish: whipped cream and freshly grated nutmeg

Crepes: Mix all ingredients together with an electric mixer. Heat crepe pan with oil to ensure crepes don't stick. Use one quarter cup of batter at a time and make crepes. Keep warm.

Filling: Mix all ingredients in saute pan and cook until bananas are soft. Spoon on filling, roll into a tube and place joined side down on a plate. *Garnish with fresh whipped cream and freshly grated nutmeg.*

*The more liquor you add to the filling, the better you will enjoy!!

CAPTAIN'S CREPES

Preparation time: 20 minutes
Cooking time: 10 minutes
Serves: 6

Chef: Kelly Reed
Yacht: Capricious

6 crepes (see below)

Filling:
   1 cup Ricotta cheese
   3 Tblsp. sugar
   1 tsp. cinnamon
   1/4 tsp. ground cloves
Syrup:
   1 cup chocolate fudge
   1/4 Grand Marnier
Garnish: fresh orange slices
   marinated in Grand Marnier

Crepes: Use Bisquick recipe for pancakes, increasing liquids by 50-75%.

Filling: Combine ingredients for filling.

Syrup: Mix together the chocolate fudge and the Grand Marnier, heat.

Spread filling on crepes, roll up, lace with syrup. *Garnish with the orange slices and serve.*

For a nice breakfast, double recipe and replace chocolate fudge with orange marmalade.

FLAMING ORANGE CREPES

Preparation time: 35 minutes   *Chef: Gina Stafford*
Cooking time: 5 minutes   *Yacht: Covenant II*
Serves: 6-8

16-20 crepes (see *Gina's Banana Crepes* on page 94)
Orange Butter:
   1/2 cup butter, softened
   1/2 cup sugar
   1 orange rind, grated
   3 Tblsp. orange juice
   1/2 cup Grand Marnier
Garnish: whipped cream

Crepes: Prepare as in **Gina's Banana Crepes** recipe. If made ahead of time, place in a pan, cover lightly with foil and reheat in a 250 degree F. oven until crepes are warm, about 15 minutes.

Orange butter: In a medium bowl beat the butter until fluffy, gradually beat in sugar, then blend in the orange rind. Gradually add the orange juice. (If preparing ahead of time, cover and refrigerate; let return to room temperature before serving.)

To serve, place a scant tablespoon of orange butter onto half of each crepe; fold in quarters and arrange slightly overlapping on a rimmed, heatproof platter. Flame the crepes by heating the Grand Marnier in a small metal pan until barely warm to touch. Ignite carefully and pour, flaming, over the crepes. Lift crepes with two forks until flames die out. Garnish with a little whipped cream.

Note: *Liqueur will not ignite if overheated.*

This dessert is spectacular and very sweet. For a nice presentation, place the platter of crepes and serving plates on the table, heat liqueur, then ignite at the table.

GINA'S BANANA CREPES

Preparation time: 30 minutes
Chilling time: 1 hour
Cooking time: 10 minutes
Serves: 8

Chef: Gina Stafford
Yacht: Covenant II

Crepes:
  1 cup flour
  2 Tblsp. powdered sugar
  3/4 cup water
  2/3 cup milk
  3 eggs
  2 Tblsp. salad oil
  1/2 tsp. vanilla extract
  1/4 tsp. salt
Filling:
  5 oz. butter
  1/3 cup brown sugar
  4 or 5 bananas (sliced)
  1 Tblsp. brandy or rum
  1/2 gallon vanilla ice cream
Garnish: whipped cream and cherries (optional)

Crepes: In a blender combine all the ingredients, process on low speed until smooth. Cover and refrigerate for 1 hour or more. Blend the batter well, then make crepes using a lightly oiled, heated 6-7 inch pan.

Filling: Melt butter in large pan, add brown sugar, bananas and brandy (or rum). Sauté on medium heat until bananas just start to get soft. Wrap one crepe around 2 scoops of ice cream, spoon the banana mixture over it and cover with whipped cream and a cherry. Repeat for all.

This is a stunning dessert and so easy to make, especially if you make the crepes ahead of time.

ORANGE FILLED CHOCOLATE CREPES WITH FUDGE SAUCE

Preparation time: 35 minutes　　　*Chef: Nancy May*
Chilling time: 1 hour　　　　　　*Yacht: Tri MyWay*
Cooking time: 15-20 minutes
Soaking time: several hours
Serves: 6

Crepes: 1 cup unbleached flour
　2 eggs
　1 cup milk
　1 Tblsp. cocoa
　2 Tblsp. powdered sugar
　Dash of salt
Filling: 4 seedless oranges
　1/3 cup Grand Marnier
　1/4 cup orange marmalade
　1/2 cup nuts, chopped
Sauce: 2 Tblsp. butter
　4oz. semi-sweet chocolate
　Reserved liquid from oranges
　3-4 Tblsp. powdered sugar

Crepes: Whip together all crepe ingredients in a blender. Refrigerate for one hour. Heat the crepe pan, then brush with melted butter. Pour in 1/4 cup of crepe batter, tilt pan until it is lightly coated. Cook about 30 seconds or until lightly browned, flip over and cook 15-20 seconds. Remove and keep warm. Repeat for each crepe.
Filling: Peel and section oranges, let soak in Grand Marnier for several hours. Strain and reserve liquid. Preheat oven to 300 degrees F. Mix in marmalade and nuts. Fill and roll crepes, place on lightly buttered tray and bake.
Sauce: Melt butter and chocolate in double boiler, add liquid and sugar. Cook on low heat. *Serve sauce over the crepes while hot.*

Tip: *Prepare crepes and soak the oranges ahead of time.*

PEACH MELBA CREPES

Preparation time: 15 minutes   *Chef: Paulette Hadley*
Chilling time: 1 hour   *Yacht: Chardonnay*
Cooking time: 20 minutes
Serves: 6-8

**1 (10 oz.) pkg. frozen raspberries or
    8 oz. raspberry sauce
1/3 cup currant jelly
3 Tblsp. butter
1/4 tsp. almond extract
1 (16 oz.) can peach slices, drained
10 scoops vanilla ice cream
10 cooked crepes (see recipe below)
1/4 cup almonds, sliced or slivered**

Thaw raspberries and force through a strainer. Combine puree or syrup, jelly, butter and extract. Bring to a boil over moderate heat. Add peaches, set aside and cool 5 minutes. Place a scoop of ice cream in each crepe, fold over, spoon sauce with peaches over crepes. Sprinkle with almonds. *Serve immediately while sauce is still warm.*

Dessert Crepes (Makes 2 cups of batter)
    **3 eggs
    1 cup milk
    3 Tblsp. butter, melted
    3/4 cup all-purpose flour
    2 Tblsp. sugar
    1/2 tsp. salt**

Combine ingredients in blender, about 1 minute. Scrape batter off sides of blender if necessary. Blend until smooth, about 30 seconds. Refrigerate one hour. Heat crepe pan, lightly butter it. Pour in small ladle of batter, tilt pan to spread evenly. Cook about 1 minute over moderately high heat, turn and cook a few more seconds. Keep warm, and proceed with Peach Melba.

Note: *Crepes freeze well. Makes enough for two charters.*

MARGOT'S "FOURSOME FONDUE"

Preparation time: 15 minutes   *Chef: Margot Drybrough*
Cooking time: 15 minutes   *Yacht: Ann-Marie II*
Serves: 4

Seasonal fruits, cut in 1 inch pieces (apples, bananas, pineapple) about 1 cup each
1/2 Sara Lee pound cake, cut in 1 inch squares
1 (6 oz.) pkg. semi-sweet chocolate morsels
1 (6 oz.) pkg. butterscotch morsels
2 (6 oz.) cans evaporated milk
2 cups marshmallow cream
Garnish: 1 cup strawberries with tops

Cut up the fruit and cake. Wash strawberries, leaving hulls on. In a saucepan heat the morsels and milk, stirring slowly until melted, add marshmallow cream and stir until well blended. Pour the warm mixture into a small, heated fondue pot. Arrange the fruit and cake on a fondue plate with dipping spears and garnish with strawberries. *Grab for the dipping spears and dig in!*

Ideal for a snack or Sunday brunch, for big appetites this is a wonderful dessert after dinner.

FRESH FRUIT FONDUE

Preparation time: 5 minutes
Chilling time: 1 hour
Serves: 6-10

Chef: Suzanne Copley
Yacht: Antiquity

Fresh fruit: melons, pineapple, strawberries, apples
2 cups sour cream
4 oz. cream cheese (softened)
1/4 cup powdered sugar
1/4 cup Kahlua

Blend well, sour cream, cream cheese, sugar and Kahlua with mixer or wire whisk. Chill for one hour. *Serve with fresh fruit such as melons, pineapple, apples and strawberries cut into bite size wedges.*

Hint: *You may use Amaretto, Frangelico, Grand Marnier, or your favorite liqueur in place of the Kahlua. This recipe can also be used as a sauce over a fresh fruit compote.*

WEST INDIAN FONDUE

Preparation time: 2 minutes
Cooking time: 10 minutes
Serves: 6-10

Chef: Jan Robinson
Yacht: Vanity

6 oz. unsweetened chocolate
1-1/2 cups sugar
1 cup whipping cream
1/2 cup butter
3 Tblsp. Crème de Cacao
Cake or fruit, cut into bite-size pieces

Combine first 4 ingredients in double boiler over warm water and stir frequently until melted, about 10 minutes. Add Crème de Cacao and blend mixture well. *Serve with cake or assorted fruit.*

PUFFED MANGO PANCAKE

Preparation time: 5 minutes   *Chef: Anna Hancock*
Cooking time: 15 minutes   *Yacht: Sly Mongoose*
Serves: 4

2 Tblsp. butter
4 eggs
3/4 cup milk
1 cup flour
1/2 tsp. salt
1 Tblsp. white sugar
2 Tblsp. butter for sauteeing
2 Tblsp. brown sugar
2 medium-size mangoes, cut into small cubes
1 Tblsp. lime juice

Preheat oven to 400 degrees F.
Melt 2 tablespoons of butter in a 12-inch ovenproof skillet in the oven. Combine eggs and milk, add flour, salt and sugar, mix well after each addition, batter should be smooth. Pour batter into the skillet and return to oven, bake for 15 minutes. In another skillet, melt butter and brown sugar, saute mangoes for 5 minutes. Add lime juice. Pour over pancake and serve!

If you don't have mangoes, other kinds of fruit can be used. If topped with fresh berries, and whipped cream it is a wonderful dessert.

FRUIT FRITTERS

Preparation time: 15 minutes   *Chef: Jan Robinson*
Cooking time: 15 minutes   *Yacht: Vanity*
Serves: 4-6

Fritter Batter (see recipe below)
1-1/4 lbs. canned peach halves, pineapple rings,
   or 1-1/2 lbs. bananas, or 3 cooking apples
Corn or peanut oil for frying
Garnish: Superfine or powdered sugar

Prepare the fritter batter. Fill a deep fryer half way up with oil, heat slowly to 375 degrees F. Drain the syrup from the canned peaches and pineapple and dry thoroughly on paper towels. If using bananas, remove skins and cut into 3 or 4 diagonal chunks; peel, core and cut the apples in slices about 1/2 inch thick.

Dip fruit into batter. Drain off excess batter; fry the fruit in hot oil for 2-3 minutes, turning fruit halfway through cooking. Fry a few pieces at a time. Drain on paper towels. Keep fritters warm in 300 degrees F. oven, until all are cooked. *Serve dredged with the superfine sugar.*

Fritter Batter:
Preparation time: 5 minutes
Resting time: 1 hour

1 cup all-purpose flour
Pinch of salt
1 Tblsp. corn oil
1/2 cup water
1 egg white

Sift flour and salt together into a bowl. Make a well in the center, add oil and water, beating until smooth. Allow the batter to rest. Beat the egg white until stiff, but not dry, then fold into batter with a rubber spatula.

ISLAND APPLE FRITTERS

Preparation time: 10 minutes   *Chef: Jan Robinson*
Cooking time: 30 minutes   *Yacht: Vanity*
Makes: about 2 dozen

2 egg yolks
1/2 cup warmed honey
1 cup yogurt
2 cups whole wheat pastry flour
1/2 tsp. nutmeg
1/2 tsp. salt
1/2 tsp. soda
1 Tblsp. melted butter
2 egg whites, beaten stiff
4 tart apples, cored and sliced 1/4 inch thick
1/2 cup oil for baking
Garnish: 1 cup maple syrup
   1/4 cup Westerhall Plantation rum* (optional)

Beat egg yolks with honey until smooth and light; add yogurt and stir until smooth. Sift together flour, nutmeg, salt and soda. Add to egg mixture. Stir in melted butter, then fold in egg whites. In a heavy iron skill, put enough oil to measure about 1/4 inch deep. Heat to 370 degrees F. or until oil starts to smoke (medium-high). Dip apple rings into batter, then bake in hot oil until golden brown on both sides. Keep fritters warm until all apples and batter have been used.Serve hot with a small pitcher of maple syrup mixed with the rum.

Hint: Fresh peaches, pears, pineapple, or bananas may be substituted for apples in this recipe.

* Westerhall Plantation Rum comes from Grenada and is made in small batches, which are never exactly alike. It has an amber color, like cognac and a lovely bouquet of caramel and vanilla. Westerhall Plantation is available and it's quite expensive, but worth it. *I love it!*

Notes

DIET DELIGHTS

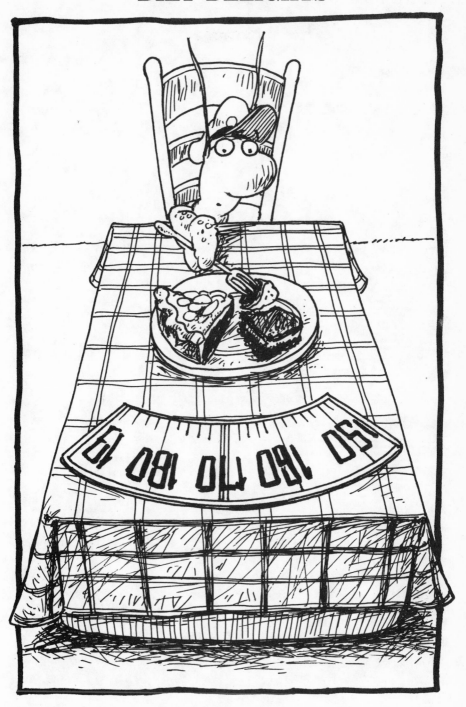

Notes

DIETER'S DREAM

Preparation time: 10 minutes   *Chef: Penny Knowles*
Cooking time: none   *Yacht: Golden Skye*
Serves: 1

1 cup whipping cream
1/2 cup sugar
1/4 cup rum
1/2 lb. chocolate, melted

Whip cream with sugar and rum. Add melted chocolate. Indulge yourself whilst sitting with your eyes shut dreaming you should really start that diet tomorrow.

OK, promise this is the last sweet thing I'll eat ... Then I'm on a diet!

BLACKBERRY RICOTTA MOUSSE
WITH CHAMBORD

Preparation time: 30 minutes   *Chef: Cathleen Govatski*
Chilling time: 6 hours or more   *Yacht: Lady Privilege*
Serves: 6-8

16 oz. Ricotta cheese, chilled
2-3 Tblsp. honey
1 Tblsp. real vanilla extract
2 cans blackberries, drained
4 Tblsp. Chambord liqueur
Garnish: chocolate shavings

With electric mixer on medium to high speed whip Ricotta
5 minutes, keep beating adding honey and vanilla. Beat to
incorporate. Fold in blackberries and Chambord. Place in
souffle dish or individual dessert dishes and chill at least
6 hours. *Garnish with chocolate shavings.*

Note: *Fast and easy – a great way to top off an Italian meal
of pasta. Low cholestrol and very little caloric content.*

Tip: *If the Ricotta is not cold when whipped it will not set
well.*

HONEY FRUIT AND YOGURT

Preparation time: 20 minutes
Chilling time: overnight
Serves: 6-8

Chef: Penny Knowles
Yacht: Golden Skye

1 cup red fruit (strawberries or raspberries)
1 cup green fruit (kiwi or white grapes)
1 cup orange fruit (mango slices or cantaloupe balls)
Thin clear honey
1 cup fresh orange juice
3 tsp. lemon juice
1/2 cup orange liqueur
1-1/2 cups plain yogurt
1/2 cup chopped nuts

Cut fruit into bite size pieces, keep grapes and berries whole. Put fruit in a bowl, sweeten with honey add orange juice, lemon juice and liqueur. Cover and chill overnight.

To serve: Sweeten the yogurt with honey and put in a bowl. Sprinkle with chopped nuts. Put bowl in the center of a serving plate. Arrange the fruit around it in a colorful pattern. Dip, eat and enjoy!

Use fresh fruit !

BAKED APPLES

Preparation time: 20 minutes　　　*Chef: Jan Robinson*
Cooking time: 45 minutes　　　　　　*Yacht: Vanity*
Serves: 4

4 medium baking apples
1/4 tsp. ground cinnamon
1/4 tsp. ground allspice
1 (12 oz.) can diet strawberry or raspberry-flavored
　carbonated beverage

Preheat oven to 350 degrees F.
Wash apples; core and quarter with peelings on. Sprinkle cut surface of apples with cinnamon and allspice. Place cut side down in a 2-quart baking dish. Pour beverage over apples. Bake for 45 minutes or until tender.

Note: *80 calories per serving. May use 1-1/2 cups low-calorie cranberry juice instead of carbonated beverage; will add 18 calories per serving.*

LITE BANANA PUDDING

Preparation time: 20 minutes　　　*Chef: Jan Robinson*
Chilling time: 20-30 minutes　　　　*Yacht: Vanity*
Serves: 4

1 (1.1 oz.) pkg. sugar-free instant vanilla pudding mix
2 cups skim milk
16 vanilla wafers
2 small bananas

Prepare pudding mix according to package directions using skim milk, chill. Line individual dessert dishes with 4 vanilla wafers each, add 1/2 sliced banana to each dish. Top with vanilla pudding.

Enjoy! A mere 180 calories per serving.

LITE FRUIT SALAD

Preparation time: 15 minutes   *Chef: Jan Robinson*
Cooking time: 1 minute (microwave)   *Yacht: Vanity*
Serves: 6

Syrup:
  2 oranges
  2 Tblsp. honey
  1/4 tsp. vanilla essence
  2 Tblsp. brandy
Fruit:
  1 or 2 kiwi fruit
  1 or 2 bananas
  1/2 or 1 fresh pineapple
  1 medium melon
  1 or 2 ripe pears
  24 grapes

Syrup: Squeeze the juice of one orange. Heat it with the honey at full power for about 1 minute, or until honey melts and mixes with the juice. Pour into a serving dish, add the vanilla and brandy.

Fruit: Prepare the selected fruits, removing seeds, pith, etc. Cut into neat small cubes and toss in the syrup. Add remaining fruit, turn gently to coat. Cover dish with plastic film to prevent fruit drying out. Marinate in the refrigerator until ready to serve.

This is a wonderful lite dessert in an interesting microwaved syrup. Serve by itself, or if you don't want to be quite so "lite", serve with yogurt, créme fraîche, whipped cream or ice cream!

LITE PECAN PIE

Preparation time: 20 minutes　　*Chef: Ninia Cunningham*
Cooking time: 35-40 minutes　　*Yacht: Iona of the Islands*
Serves: 6-8

9 inch pie shell, uncooked
5-1/2 Tblsp. lite margarine
1 cup light brown sugar
4 eggs
1 cup lite syrup
2 Tblsp. white vinegar
1 Tblsp. dark rum
Pinch of salt
1-1/2 cups pecans
Garnish: lite whipped cream

Preheat oven to 425 degrees F.
Cream sugar and margarine. Beat in eggs one at a time. Add syrup, vinegar, rum and salt. Pour into pie crust and bake for 30 minutes, reduce heat to 375 degrees F. when crust is browned. Bake until top of pie is firm and a knife inserted comes out clean, about 5-10 minutes more. *Serve warm or chilled with lite whipped cream. Honestly, it's lite!*

Dieting !

LITE CREAMY RICE PUDDING

Preparation time: 15 minutes
Cooking time: 45 minutes
Serves: 6

Chef: Jan Robinson
Yacht: Vanity

2 egg yolks
1/4 cup plus 1/4 cup sugar
1 cup 2% low-fat milk, scalded
1/2 tsp. ground cinnamon
1/8 tsp. ground nutmeg
1 tsp. vanilla extract
3 cups 2% low-fat milk
3 cups cooked long-grain rice, (cooked without salt or fat)
3/4 cup raisins

Beat egg yolks in a medium bowl until thick and lemon colored, gradually add 1/4 cup sugar, beat mixture 1 minute. Gradually add scalded milk, whisk until well blended. Pour mixture into a medium size saucepan, and place over medium heat; cook until thickened, stirring constantly with a wire whisk. Remove from heat, stir in cinnamon, nutmeg, and vanilla extract. Set aside.

Bring 3 cups of milk to a boil over medium heat in a large, heavy saucepan, stirring frequently. Reduce heat to medium-low; add cooked rice and remaining 1/4 cup sugar. Cook 30 minutes or until milk is absorbed, stirring frequently. Fold in egg yolk mixture and raisins. *Serve warm or chilled. (Only 163 calories per 1/2 cup serving.)*

Hint: *To scald milk, place in a heavy saucepan, and cook over medium heat to 180 degrees F. or until tiny bubbles form around edges of pan.*

LOW CALORIE OATMEAL COOKIES

Preparation time: 15 minutes   *Chef: Jan Robinson*
Cooking time: 20 minutes   *Yacht: Vanity*
Makes: about 30

3 bananas, mashed
2 cups uncooked quick-cooking oats
1/2 cup raisins
1/3 cup reduced-calorie margarine, melted
1/4 cup skim milk
1 tsp vanilla extract

Preheat oven to 350 degrees F.
Combine all ingredients, beating well. Let stand 5 minutes so oats will absorb moisture. Drop dough by heaping teaspoonfuls onto ungreased cookie sheets and bake for 15-20 minutes. Let stand a few minutes on cookie sheets, then transfer to a wire rack to cool completely. *Each cookie has about 45 calories.*

HEALTH FOOD NUT'S DESSERT

Preparation time: 15 minutes   *Chef: Jan Robinson*
Serves: 4   *Yacht: Vanity*

2 cups fresh fruits, any combination
3 Tblsp. rum
1/2 teaspoon each cinnamon and nutmeg
6 Tblsp. granola
8 oz. yogurt, plain or flavored
6 tsp. nutmeg spiced wheat germ

Marinate the cut up fruit in rum spiced with cinnamon and nutmeg. Place a spoonful of granola in a custard cup. Add fruit and top with a healthy dollop of yogurt. Sprinkle with the spiced wheat germ.

Note: *Its better to prepare this dessert ahead of time to allow the fruit to marinate in the rum. If you're not so interested in being healthy, add more rum!*

LOW CHOLESTEROL STICKY BUNS

Preparation time: 1 hour
Rising time: 1-2 hours
Cooking time: 25-35 minutes
Serves: 8-12

Chef: Laura Flintoff
Yacht: Icebear

1 cup plus 3/4 cup corn oil
1 cup evaporated skim milk
1 pkg. yeast, dissolved in 1/2 cup warm water
1/3 cup plus 3 Tblsp. granulated sugar
3 eggs or 3/4 cup Egg Beaters
1 tsp. salt
1-1/2 lbs. (approx.) all-purpose flour
3 Tblsp. plus 1 cup brown sugar
2 tsp. cinnamon
1 cup plus 1-1/2 cup pecans
3/4 cup raisins
1/2 cup honey
1/3 cup rum (dark)
Parchment paper

Preheat oven to 350 degrees F.
Dough: Warm 1 cup oil and milk, add yeast mix and 1/3 cup sugar, let bloom. Add eggs, gradually add salt and flour. Knead and let rise. **Filling:** Process 3 Tblsp. each brown and granulated sugar, 2 tsp. cinnamon, 1 cup pecans, 3/4 cup raisins, set aside. **Topping:** Combine 1 cup brown sugar, honey, 3/4 cup oil, rum, 1-1/2 cup pecan halves. Roll dough to 1/4 inch thick, spread filling on top, roll out like a Jelly Roll. Cut to 1-1/2 inch slices.

Grease bottom of straight sided pan, line with parchment paper, let hang over two ends of pan. Pour topping into pan, place slices 1/2 inch apart on top. Spray with Pam, cover with a bag. Let dough rise 1-2 hours or until double in bulk. Bake, when done place a cookie sheet on top of pan and invert quickly. Remove paper, separate and serve.

This is a nice treat for someone on a low cholesterol diet who has a sweet tooth!

MINTED FRUIT DIP

Preparation time: 10 minutes　　　*Chef: Jan Robinson*
Cooking time: none　　　　　　　　*Yacht: Vanity*
Makes: 1 cup

1 (8 oz.) carton lime or lemon yogurt
1 Tblsp. green Creme de Menthe
Fruit: grapefruit sections, sliced bananas, pineapple,
**　fresh strawberries, sliced peaches, honeydew or**
**　cantaloupe**
Ladyfingers, optional

Combine yogurt and Creme de Menthe in small bowl and mix until thoroughly blended. *Serve as a dip for assorted fresh fruit or ladyfingers.*

PARADISE PEARS

Preparation time: 10 minutes　　*Chef: Margot Drybrough*
Cooking time: none　　　　　　　*Yacht: Anne-Marie II*
Serves: 4

1 (6 oz.) pkg. reduced calorie cream cheese
1/4 tsp. ground cinnamon
Dash ground nutmeg
1 large can Bartlett pears, unsweetened
Garnish: sprig of fresh mint

Blend together softened cream cheese, cinnamon and nutmeg. Drain pears, reserve syrup. Put 2 halves in each bowl. (The large cans usually have 8 small halves.) Spoon even amounts of mixture into the center of each pear half. Pour a little juice into each bowl and garnish with a sprig of fresh mint. Refreshing!

This is a great alternative to rich, fattening desserts. No guilt trips here!

ORANGE CHERRY DELIGHT

Preparation time: 10 minutes   *Chef: Jan Robinson*
Chilling time: 30 minutes   *Yacht: Vanity*
Serves: 4

1 env. unflavored gelatin
1 cup water
3 oz. unsweetened frozen orange-juice concentrate
1 Tblsp. honey
1-1/2 cups unsweetened frozen cherries

In a small saucepan, sprinkle gelatin over water. Set aside to soften for 5 minutes. Dissolve gelatin over medium heat stirring constantly. Pour into a blender and process with remaining ingredients until liquefied. Pour into dessert dishes and chill until set. *This is a good one, only about 84 calories per serving!*

PEACHY PARFAIT

Preparation time: 15 minutes   *Chef: Jan Robinson*
Cooking time: none   *Yacht: Vanity*
Serves: 4

2 (8-oz.) containers peach low-fat yogurt
4 large, fresh, medium peaches, sliced and de-stoned
Garnish: 4 strawberries with tops

Layer yogurt and peach slices in 4 dessert or parfait glasses, ending with yogurt on top. Top each with a strawberry.

Only about 150 calories per creamy serving!

Note: *You may use any fruit and complimentary flavor yogurt.*

STRAWBERRY ICE

Preparation time: 5 minutes   *Chef: Jan Robinson*
Freezing time: 1-2 hours   *Yacht:Vanity*
Serves: 6

4 cups fresh strawberries
1/2 cup pineapple juice
1/4 cup honey
Garnish: strawberry slices

Combine all ingredients in a food processor until smooth. Pour mixture into a 1-1/2 quart casserole dish. Cover and freeze until slushy, about 20-30 minutes. Return mixture to food processor and process until smooth. Freeze until firm (an hour or so).*To serve: scoop into stemmed dessert dishes - like a parfait - and garnish with fresh strawberry slices.*

Note: *This fruity dessert has only about 82 calories per serving. If you use 8 packages of sugar substitute in place of the honey, the calorie count goes down to about 47 calories per serving.*

SUGARLESS ALMOND COOKIES

Preparation time: 20 minutes
Cooking time: 20 minutes
Makes: 30 cookies

Chef: Jan Robinson
Yacht: Vanity

1/4 cup plus 2 Tblsp. reduced-calorie margarine
1 tsp powdered sugar substitute
1 egg yolk
1/2 tsp. almond extract
1/4 tsp. vanilla extract
1/4 tsp. lemon extract
1 cup all-purpose flour
1/2 tsp. baking powder
1/8 tsp. salt

Preheat oven to 300 degrees F.

Cream margarine and sugar substitute in a medium bowl until light and fluffy. Add egg yolk and extracts; beat well. Combine flour, baking powder and salt; add to creamed mixture, beating well. Shape dough into 1 inch balls; place 2 inches apart on ungreased cookie sheets. Press each with a fork to flatten. Bake for 20 minutes or until edges begin to brown. *Remove cookies to wire racks and cool completely.*

Each cookie about 33 calories.

SUGARLESS DATE BARS

Preparation time: 15 minutes   *Chef: Jan Robinson*
Cooking time: 3 minutes (micorwave)   *Yacht: Vanity*
Chilling time: 30 minutes
Makes: 24

1 (8 oz.) pkg. dates, pitted and chopped
1 Tblsp. all-purpose flour
1/2 cup water, boiling
3/4 cup unsweetened coconut, grated
1/2 cup reduced calorie margarine
1-1/2 tsp. powdered sugar substitute
2-1/2 cups uncooked instant oats
1/2 tsp. vanilla extract
Vegetable cooking spray

In a large mixing bowl, combine dates and flour; toss lightly to coat. Pour boiling water over dates, add coconut, margarine and sugar, stirring well. Microwave on high for 2-3 minutes or until thickened, stirring at 1 minute intervals. Add oats and vanilla to date mixture. Spray a 9-inch square baking dish with vegetable cooking spray and spoon in mixture, press evenly into bottom of pan. Cover and refrigerate until set. *Cut into 24 bars and store in an airtight container in the refrigerator.*

Note: *One bar is about 80 calories.*

SIMPLE PARTY DESSERT

Preparation time: 20 minutes   *Chef: Jan Robinson*
Chilling time: 30 minutes   *Yacht: Vanity*
Serves: 10-14

1 large melon, cantaloupe, Persian or watermelon
And whatever fruits you have on hand
Lemon juice
Grated coconut, chopped dates, raisins and
    chopped unsalted nuts (any kind)
Garnish: Cinnamon, nutmeg, allspice, ginger,
    anise or cardamon

Cut melon in half and scoop out meat with melon ball scoop (save shells). Prepare chosen fruit and cut into chunks, sprinkle with lemon juice to keep the fruit looking fresh and to add a bit of tang. Combine melon balls with fruit and put back in shells. Cover and chill until ready to serve. *To serve: Place shells on large platter; sprinkle with your selected blend of spices and surround with small bowls of coconut, nuts, raisins and chopped dates.*

Note: One cup of any combination of fresh fruits, plus 1 Tblsp. of nuts or raisins, averages about 100 calories per serving.

TANGY LEMON-LIME FLUFF

Preparation time: 15 minutes   *Chef: Jan Robinson*
Chilling time: 20-30 minutes   *Yacht: Vanity*
Serves: 4

1 (3 oz.) pkg. sugar-free lime gelatin
3/4 cup boiling water
1/4 cup fresh lemon juice
1 (8 oz.) can crushed pineapple, drained
1-1/2 cups plain low-fat yogurt
Zest of lime
Zest of lemon
2 Tblsp. Graham cracker crumbs

Combine gelatin, boiling water, and lemon juice, stir until dissolved. Set aside and let cool. Combine pineapple, yogurt, and zest, fold into gelatin and pour into a 1-1/2 quart casserole dish. Sprinkle with graham cracker crumbs, and chill until firm. *Cut into squares and serve.*

Just near 96 calories and 126 mg. sodium per serving for this delightfully refreshing dessert.

RECIPE FOR DISASTER

Preparation time: 1 week
Cooking time: 1 week
Serves: 3 crew

Chef: Vanessa Owen
Yacht: Endless Summer II

1 charter boat
8 charter guests
No Dramamine
25 knot winds
Generous helping of waves
Liberal rain and clouds
1 desire to visit Anegada
Garnish: several soothing words from the crew

Start with a charter boat, add guests who have never sailed (very important) and forget to bring along the Dramamine. Combine winds, waves, cloudy day and sail to Anegada. Add a day to the holiday – if separation occurs, drop sails and motor back to port.

Notes

FROZEN AND CHILLED DESSERTS

Notes

BUTTERSCOTCH PECAN FUDGE GATEAU

Preparation time: 20 minutes   *Chef: Fiona Dugdale*
Chilling time: 8 hours   *Yacht: Promenade*
Serves: 8-10

6 oz. unsalted butter
3/4 cup golden or dark Karo syrup
1 pkg. wheatmeal cookies
1-1/2 cups pitted dates
1/2 cup candied cherries
1-1/2 cups pecans
Garnish: whipped cream

In a saucepan melt butter and blend in syrup. Crumble cookies. Finely chop cherries and dates. Crush and toast pecans. Mix all ingredients together. Press mixture into a plastic wrap lined loaf pan. Chill at least 8 hours or overnight. *Serve sliced with whipped cream.*

CHOCOLATE RICOTTA

Preparation time: 15 minutes   *Chef: Marilyn Stenberg*
Cooking time: none   *Yacht: Sabina D*
Serves: 4

2 oz. semi-sweet chocolate
1-1/2 tsp. freshly grated nutmeg
2 cups Ricotta cheese
1/2 cup powdered sugar
Vanilla extract or rum to taste
Garnish: chocolate curls and whipped cream

Using the fine side of a grater, grate the chocolate onto wax paper. Repeat with the nutmeg (don't wash the grater in between). Mix the cheese, sugar, nutmeg and chocolate until blended, add vanilla or rum. Cover with plastic and refrigerate until needed.

CHOCOLATE MARQUISE
& CREME ANGLAISE

Preparation time: 20 minutes
Chilling time: overnight
Serves: 10

Chef: Fiona Dugdale
Yacht: Promenade

Chocolate Marquise:
   12 oz. bittersweet chocolate
   1/2 cup sugar
   1 cup butter
   1/2 cup cocoa
   6 eggs, separated
Creme Anglaise:
   2 cups milk
   3 egg yolks
   1 Tblsp. sugar
   1 tsp. vanilla
Garnish: fresh strawberries

Chocolate Marquise: Break up chocolate, pulse in a food processor with sugar. Melt and pour hot butter through feed tube of processor with the motor running. Add cocoa and egg yolks, pulse. Whip egg whites and fold into chocolate mixture. Line a loaf pan with plastic wrap, pour in mixture, chill 8 hours or overnight.

Creme Anglaise: Boil milk. Mix together egg yolks and sugar, while stirring, pour mixture into milk. Cook until slightly thickened, add vanilla.

To serve: Spread some Creme Anglaise on each dessert plate and place a 1/2-inch slice of Marquise on top. Garnish with fresh strawberries cut into fans for special occasions.

My husband, David, calls this "Sin on a Blanket".

SUMMER PUDDING

Preparation time: 20 minutes   *Chef: Penny Knowles*
Chilling time: 2-3 hours   *Yacht: Golden Skye*
Serves: 6

4 cups mixed berries (frozen or canned)
10 slices of raisin bread
Sugar if necessary

Defrost fruit (using frozen fruit is better than canned). Sweeten with sugar to your taste. Add any extra liquid so that there is enough to cover the fruit (a drop or two of orange liqueur is nice). Cut the crusts off the bread and line a 6 cup pudding bowl. Pour in the fruit and just enough liquid to keep it moist. Top with remaining bread slices. Place a small plate on top of the pudding as a weight. Chill for several hours. *Turn out of the bowl onto a plate to serve.*

Hint: *This is a traditional English recipe. Any red berry fruits such as raspberries, strawberries, black currants, and blueberries can be used. If you use white bread, flavor the fruit with a little cinnamon.*

_Yep, he had too much of that exotic
pudding!

CHOCOLATE MINT PUDDING

Preparation time: 20 minutes
Cooking time: 5 minutes
Chilling time: 3 hours
Serves: 6-8

Chef: Karen Roest
Yacht: Rising Sun 64

1 bag Pepperidge Farm Mint Milano Cookies, crumbled
3 Tblsp. milk
1 pkg. semi-sweet cooking chocolate
5 eggs, separated
1 tsp. vanilla
3 Tblsp. Creme de Menthe
Garnish: grated chocolate, mint leaves

In a serving bowl place the crumbled cookies. Melt chocolate with milk over low heat until smooth, cool. Add Creme de Menthe to chocolate. Beat egg yolks until well blended, add vanilla and mix well. Beat egg whites until fluffy. Add yolks to chocolate mixture and fold in egg whites. Pour over cookies and refrigerate until set, about 3 hours. *Garnish with grated chocolate and mint leaves, or cover with whipped cream.*

This dessert is always well liked, you may have guests wanting to lick the bowl!

Hint: *Instead of making chocolate pudding, use chocolate pudding mix. Add Creme de Menthe to mixture.*

COCONUT PUDDING IN A CLOUD

Preparation time: 20 minutes
Chilling time: 20 minutes
Serves: 6

Chef: Beth Avore
Yacht: Perfection

1 large pkg. instant vanilla pudding
Milk
1/4 cup Ron Ricardo Coconut Rum
1/2 to 1 cup grated coconut, toasted
Cool Whip
Garnish: coconut, toasted and grated

Prepare pudding as directed on box, substituting 1/4 cup rum for some of the milk. Add coconut and set aside. Line 6 dessert cups with 1/2 to 3/4 inch of Cool Whip, making a slight hollow and extending a little beyond the rim of the cups. Pour pudding into the hollows in the Cool Whip. Sprinkle with toasted coconut. Refrigerate until firm before serving.

Hint: *Suppliment with a variety of Pepperidge Farm Distinctive Cookies for added flair.*

PUDDING CREMEUX

Preparation time: 10 minutes   *Chef: Jolyne Grondin*
Cooking time: 10 minutes   *Yacht: Stowaway*
Chilling time: 3 hours
Serves: 4

2 Tblsp. water
1 cup sugar
2 cups milk
1-1/2 Tblsp. cornstarch
2 eggs, beaten
1 Tblsp. vanilla
2 Tblsp. Tia Maria
Garnish: whipped cream and butter cookies

Mix water and 1/2 cup sugar in saucepan, cook on medium heat until caramelized. Heat 1 cup milk in saucepan. Add caramelized mixture while stirring milk. Mix cornstarch and remaining sugar, add to remaining milk, pour all into the hot milk mixture. Cook 2 minutes on low heat. Add beaten eggs, vanilla and Tia Maria. Stir and cook for 3 to 4 minutes on low heat until the mixture thickens. Spoon into dessert dishes and chill 3 hours or until serving. *Serve topped with whipped cream and some butter cookies on the side.*

To freeze dollops of whipped cream: drop heaping spoonfuls onto chilled baking sheet, swirling tops with tip of spoon. Put into freezer. When frozen, lift mounds with a spatula and store in sealed plastic bag up to 3 months. Place atop dessert a few minutes before serving to allow cream to thaw.

ALMOND CREME SAUCE
WITH FRESH FRUIT

Preparation time: 5 minutes   *Chef: Jan Robinson*
Chilling time: 30 minutes   *Yacht: Vanity*
Serves: 4-6

1 cup sour cream
3 Tblsp. powdered sugar
1-1/2 Tblsp. Amaretto liqueur
1 tsp. almond extract
Strawberries, pineapple, bananas, or your choice
Garnish: 1/2 cup blueberies (thawed if frozen)

Combine first 4 ingredients in small mixing bowl and stir well to blend. Cover and chill until ready to use. *Serve over fresh fruit and sprinkle blueberries over top.*

Light and refreshing.

SWEET AVOCADO CREAM

Preparation time: 5 minutes   *Chef: Jan Robinson*
Freezing time: 1 hour   *Yacht: Vanity*
Serves: 4

2 large ripe avocados, peeled and seeded
1/2 cup milk
1/2 cup sugar or to taste
1/2 tsp. cinnamon

Combine all ingredients in medium bowl and beat until smooth. Spoon into individual freezer proof goblets or dessert dishes. Cover and freeze until thoroughly chilled and firm, about 1 hour, in a good freezer!

AMARETTO CHANTILLY

Preparation time: 20 minutes   *Chef: Jan Robinson*
Freezing time: 3 hours   *Yacht: Vanity*
Serves: 8

3-1/4 cups miniature marshmallows
2/3 cup Amaretto
1 Tblsp. lemon juice
1/4 tsp. almond extract
1/2 cup maraschino cherries, chopped
2 cups whipping cream
2 Tblsp. pistachios or almonds, finely chopped

In the top of a double boiler combine marshmallows and
Amaretto, bring water to a boil. Cook until marshmallows
melt, stirring occasionally. Stir in lemon juice, almond
extract and cherries. Cool slightly. Beat cream until soft
peaks form, fold into marshmallow mixture. Spoon into
individual serving dishes and sprinkle with nuts. *Cover
and freeze.*

DREAM CLOUD

Preparation time: 10 minutes   *Chef: Kate Chivas*
Cooking time: none   *Yacht: Tri World*
Serves: as many as you like

Cool Whip (regular size)
1/3 cup Amaretto or Kahlua
Stella Dora cookie sticks and/or vanilla
   and chocolate wafers

Mix Cool Whip and your choice of liqueur together. Put into
a serving bowl. Place the bowl on a platter and surround
with cookies. *Delicious!*

Hint: *You may add more liqueur to the Cool Whip until you
get the consistency you like.*

CREME BRULE

Preparation time: 10 minutes
Cooking time: 25 minutes
Chilling time: 20 minutes
Serves: 8

Chef: Fiona Dugdale
Yacht: Promenade

Custard:
  6 egg yolks
  1/2 cup sugar
  1 tsp. vanilla
  1-1/2 cups heavy cream
  1-1/2 cups light cream
Topping:
  1 cup sugar
  1/4 cup water

Preheat oven to 300 degrees F.
Custard: Blend together egg yolks and sugar. Add vanilla and pour over cream and mix well. Strain into a large measuring jug. Pour mixture into 8 individual ramekin or soufflé dishes. Set in a pan containing 1 inch of water. Bake custards about 25 minutes or until just set. Cool and refrigerate.

Topping: Dissolve sugar and water, boil until caramelized, continue boiling until the mixture turns dark golden brown. Pour a little over each brûlé. *Reserve 2 tablespoons of the caramel, pour into a foil pie tin and refrigerate. When cold crush and sprinkle over brûlés.*

Note: *Jan from* **Vanity** *suggests saving the egg whites to make a Paradise Pavlova. See page 215 for the recipe!*

BANANA GELATO

Preparation time: 10 minutes   *Chef: Ronnie Hochman*
Cooking time: 5 minutes   *Yacht: Illusion II*
Freezing time: 1-2 hours
Serves: 6

1 env. unflavored gelatin
1 cup nonfat dry milk powder
1/2 cup sugar
2 cups reconstituted nonfat dry milk
1 cup ripe bananas, mashed (about 3)
1 tsp. vanilla
Garnish: banana slices and mint leaves

Mix gelatin, milk powder and sugar in a medium saucepan, stir in reconstituted milk. Using medium heat, stir constantly until gelatin dissolves. Cool, stir in bananas and vanilla. Freeze until firm. *Before serving beat with a mixer to smooth and garnish with bananas and mint leaves.Great for boat freezers, doesn't have to be frozen solid.*

CHILLED CARIBBEAN BANANAS

Preparation time: 15 minutes   *Chef: Fiona Dugdale*
Chilling time: 1 hour   *Yacht: Promenade*
Serves: 8

1/4 cup almonds, flaked
8 bananas
3 Tblsp. rum
1 cup heavy cream
3 Tblsp. Kahlua

Brown almonds and set aside. Peel and slice bananas diagonally into 8 dessert glasses, sprinkle with rum. Whip cream and stir in Kahlua. Spoon Kahlua and cream mixture over bananas. *Sprinkle with almonds and chill.*

ICE CREAM DELIGHT

Preparation time: 30 minutes   *Chef: Wendy Smith*
Freezing time: 2-3 hours   *Yacht: Hiya*
Serves: 6

2 cups vanilla ice cream
2 cups raspberry ice cream
Fresh blueberries, strawberries and raspberries
Grand Marnier
Cognac

Soften ice creams and fold together. Cut up the fresh fruits and fold into ice creams. Add Grand Marnier and/or Cognac to taste. Freeze until the ice cream is firm.*Tasty and easy if you are lucky enough to have a great freezer.*

POT de CREME

Preparation time: 5 minutes   *Chef: Gretchen Fater*
Cooking time: 2 minutes   *Yacht: Marantha*
Chilling time: 30 minutes
Serves: 6

1 cup chocolate chip morsels
1 tsp. salt
2 Tblsp. sugar
2 eggs
3/4 cup milk, barely boiling
1 tsp. vanilla
4 Tblsp. Creme de Menthe, Amaretto or Grand Marnier

Put first five ingredients in blender on high for 2 minutes. Flavor with vanilla and liqueur of your choice. Pour into dessert cups, cover with plastic wrap and chill until firm.

Smooth, heavenly chocolate!

ICE CREAM CAKE

Preparation time: 20 minutes　　　　　*Chef: Jan Robinson*
Freezing time: 2 hours　　　　　　　　*Yacht: Vanity*
Serves: 12

1 angel food cake
1/2 gallon vanilla ice cream
1 (6-1/2 oz) package thin mints, chopped
1 cup pecans, chopped
1 tsp. peppermint extract

Slice cake into 3 layers. In a large mixing bowl, combine rest of the ingredients. Place 1 layer of cake on a serving plate and ice with ice cream mixture. Top with next layer and continue adding ice cream mixture, ending up with ice cream mixture on top. Freeze immediately for at least 2 hours.

Note: *If you make more than one day ahead, wrap tightly after the ice cream hardens. For ease in cutting, run your knife under the hot water.*

BLACK FOREST MOUSSE

Preparation time: 15 minutes
Chilling time: 1 hour
Serves: 4

Chef: Christy Clifford
Yacht: Southern Cruz

1 pkg. chocolate mousse
2 Tblsp. dark rum
1 Tblsp. powdered sugar
1 cup cherry pie filling, chilled
1 cup whipped cream
Garnish: top with chocolate shavings or
Hersheys chocolate powder

In a bowl make chocolate mousse as directed on package and add 1 tablespoon of dark rum, chill 1 hour. Mix whipped cream, 1 tablespoon dark rum and 1 tablespoon of powdered sugar, chill for 1 hour. Chill can of cherry pie filling. *To serve: in 4 parfait glasses layer chocolate mousse, whipped cream, cherry filling, whipped cream, chocolate mousse, whipped cream. Sprinkle with shaved dark chocolate (or chocolate powder) and top with a cherry.*

BLENDER CHOCOLATE MOUSSE

Preparation time: 15 minutes   *Chef: Paulette Hadley*
Chillng time: 30 minutes   *Yacht: Chardonnay*
Serves: 6

1/3 cup hot coffee
1 (6 oz.) pkg. semi-sweet chocolate morsels
4 eggs at room temperature, separated
Garnish: 2 Tblsp. Creme de Cacao,
   almonds, toasted and sliced

Combine coffee and chocolate morsels in a blender until smooth. Add egg yolks and Creme de Cacao, blend 1 minute. Beat egg whites until stiff peaks form. Fold in chocolate mixture. Spoon into stemmed glasses or individual serving dishes, chill until set. *To serve: top with whipped cream and almonds. Very easy!*

STRAWBERRY AND BANANA MOUSSE

Preparation time: 5 minutes   *Chef: Jean Crook*
Chilling time: 15 minutes   *Yacht: Dileas*
Serves: 4-6

1 cup frozen strawberries, unsweetened
2 ripe bananas
3 Tblsp. orange juice
1 Tblsp. plain yogurt
Garnish: whole strawberries

Puree all ingredients together in an electric blender until creamy and smooth. Pour into small bowls and garnish with a strawberry. *Chill until serving.*

ICED DELIGHT

Preparation time: 5 minutes
Cooking time: none
Serves: 4-6

Chef: Jan Robinson
Yacht: Vanity

1 (12-oz.) pkg. frozen raspberries, thawed
3 Tblsp. cherry-flavored liqueur
lime sherbet or vanilla ice cream
Garnish: mint leaves

Place raspberries in blender or food processor and puree. Stir in liqueur. *To serve: Pour puree over scoops of lime sherbet or vanilla ice cream. Garnish with mint leaves.*

QUICK SHERBET

Preparation time: 5 minutes
Serves: 4

Chef: Jan Robinson
Yacht: Vanity

1 pint tangerine or orange sherbet
1 (11 oz.) can Mandarin oranges, drained
Curaçao liqueur to taste
Garnish: mint leaves

Scoop sherbet into dessert dishes. Arrange orange Mandarin segments over top. Sprinkle with liqueur. *Garnish with mint.*

CARIBBEAN DELIGHT

Preparation time: 5 minutes　　　　*Chef: Jan Robinson*
Cooking time: 8 minutes　　　　　*Yacht: Vanity*
Chilling time: 2 hours
Serves: 6

2 Tblsp. flour
2 Tblsp. cornstarch
Juice of 1 large lemon (about 1/4 cup)
1 (20 oz.) can crushed pineapple in its own juice and
1 (8 oz.) can crushed pineapple in its own juice
3 eggs, separated
1/2 cup sugar
1-1/2 tsp. lemon peel
1/2 tsp. baking powder
Garnish: whipped cream

Blend flour, cornstarch and lemon juice in 2 quart saucepan until smooth. Add pineapple, egg yolks, sugar, and lemon peel, mix well. Bring to a boil over medium-high heat, stirring constantly until thickened, about 5 minutes. Remove from heat and let cool slightly. Beat egg whites with baking powder until stiff peaks form, fold into pineapple. Cover and refrigerate until set, about 2 hours. *To serve: spoon into bowls and top pudding with dollops of whipped cream.*

To prevent whipped cream from becoming thin after sitting, add one teaspoon unflavored gelatin before whipping.

CHOCOLATE PARFAIT PERFECTION

Preparation time: 30 minutes
Chilling time: 15 minutes
Serves: 6

Chef: Beth Avore
Yacht: Perfection

Chocolate mousse:
 1/2 cup sugar
 3 egg yolks
 1/2 lb. unsweetend chocolate, melted
 5 egg whites, at room temperature
1-2 cup Oreo cookies, crumbled
Cool Whip or whipped cream
Garnish: cookie crumbs or chocolate shavings

In a mixing bowl beat sugar, yolks and melted chocolate, blend well and cool. Beat egg whites until very stiff, fold gently into chocolate mixture. In parfait glasses (or champagne flutes), layer cookie crumbs, mousse and Cool Whip (or whipped cream), repeat until you have 6 layers. Chill 15 minutes or until ready to serve. *Before serving, garnish with cookie crumbs or chocolate shavings.*

Note: *This is best served with a light meal as it is very rich. Also great with coffee and cordials.*

Best results for whipped cream: before whipping, chill bowl, beaters and cream till very cold.

RASPBERRY PARFAIT

Preparation time: 15 minutes   *Chef: Fiona Dugdale*
Cooking time: none   *Yacht: Promenade*
Serves: 8

4 egg whites
1 cup sugar
2 cups heavy cream
2 lbs. frozen raspberries

Beat egg whites until stiff. Add sugar one spoonful at a time. Continue beating until a meringue forms with stiff peaks. Whip cream until thick and fold into meringue. Fold in raspberries while in a semi-frozen state. *Pour into individual glasses and serve.*

Hint: *This is best if served immediately or up to one hour after preparation. If made ahead of time, keep the parfaits well chilled. Try different fruits for variation, strawberries and peaches work well. Also, try plain yogurt instead of whipped cream.*

Meringues prepared on a cloudy, rainy, or humid day will absorb moisture from the air and become soft and sticky. If baked ones become sticky, reheat in 200 degree F. oven for 30 minutes to 1 hour.

CREAMY STRAWBERRY MOLD

Preparation time: 5 minutes
Cooking time: 2 minutes
Chilling time: 1 hour
Serves: 6

Chef: Jean Crook
Yacht: Dileas

1 pkg. (3 oz.) strawberry gelatin
1 cup water, boiling
2 cups ice cream, strawberry or vanilla
2 cups miniature marshmallows
Garnish: fresh fruit (berries, peaches, pears) and
whipped cream

In a medium size mixing bowl, dissolve the gelatin in boiling water. Add ice cream and stir until melted. Chill until mixture has thickened. Fold in marshmallows. Pour into a lightly oiled 4 cup mold and chill until firm. *To serve, unmould onto a serving plate, garnish with your favorite fruit and whipped cream.*

If a molded gelatin dessert does not come out cleanly, use one of the cook's best makeover friends—whipped cream to cover the damaged surface.

CHILLED AMARETTO SOUFFLE

Preparation time: 20 minutes
Chilling time: 30 minutes
Serves: 6

Chef: John Freeman
Yacht: Solid Gold, Too

3 large eggs, separated
1/2 cup powdered sugar
Juice of 1 lemon
1-1/2 pkgs. unflavored gelatin, dissolved
2 Tblsp. water
1/4 cup ground almonds, lightly toasted
3/4 cup whipped cream
Garnish: chocolate shavings and whipped cream

Prepare 6 individual souffle dishes or 1 medium dish by lining the sides with wax paper (allow 1 inch extra in height). In a saucepan over warm water whisk egg yolks, sugar and 1/4 of the lemon juice until pale and thick. Dissolve gelatin in water, add remaining lemon juice. Add to the egg yolk mixture, whisk together and allow to cool. Beat egg whites until stiff, fold in almonds. Fold whipped cream mixture into yolk mixture followed by the whites mixture. Pour into dishes, allow to set in the refrigerator.

To serve: remove paper sides, coat sides with chocolate shavings and decorate with whipped cream.

FROZEN LIQUEUR SOUFFLE

Preparation time: 15 minutes
Freezing time: 4 hours
Serves: 8

Chef: Allison Moir
Yacht: Pride of Lyn

6 egg yolks
3/4 cup sugar
2 cups whipping cream
6 Tblsp. Grand Marnier
Garnish: whipped cream, chocolate shavings

Beat egg yolks, add the sugar gradually and beat until the sugar has dissolved and the mixture is thick and lemon colored. Whip the cream and fold in. Stir in liqueur. Spoon into dessert glasses or bowls. Freeze for at least 4 hours. Remove 20 minutes before serving. *Serve with sweetened whipped cream and chocolate shavings.*

Note: *Can be frozen up to one week. Another idea is to serve between meringues with chocolate sauce on top. See recipe for* **Meringues** *on page 81.*

LEMON SOUFFLE WITH
RASPBERRY SAUCE GRAND MARNIER

Preparation time: 30 minutes   *Chef: Paulette Hadley*
Chilling time: 3 hours   *Yacht: Chardonnay*
Serves: 6-8

2 envs. unflavored gelatin
1/2 cup cold water
8 eggs, separated
1 cup lemon juice
2 cups sugar
1/2 tsp. salt
1-1/2 tsp. lemon rind, grated
1-1/2 pints heavy cream

Sprinkle gelatin over water and let stand. Beat egg yolks with 1 cup of sugar until light and fluffy. In a double boiler combine the egg yolk mixture, lemon juice and salt. Cook, stirring constantly, over boiling water until thickened and custard-like. Add gelatin and lemon rind, stirring constantly. Turn into a large bowl to cool slightly. Beat egg whites until stiff, add 3/4 to 1 cup sugar and beat until firm peaks form, then fold into custard. Whip the cream and fold into custard. Refrigerate for 3 hours or more. *Best if served within 10 hours.*

Raspberry Sauce:
   1 (10 oz.) pkg. frozen raspberries
   Sugar to taste
   2-3 Tblsp. Grand Marnier or Cointreau

Defrost raspberries. Blend raspberries with liqueur and sugar in a blender. Strain and serve in sauce bowl.

WINE GELEE

Preparation time: 20 minutes
Cooking time: 5 minutes
Chilling time: 2 hours
Serves: 6

Chef: Ninia Cunningham
Yacht: Iona of the Islands

1-1/4 cups water
1 Tblsp. plain gelatine
Pared rind of 1 orange
Pared rind of 1/2 lemon
Pared rind of 1/2 lime
3/4 cup sugar
1-1/2 cups red wine
1 cup black or green grapes, seedless if possible
Garnish: Sugared Grapes (see below)

Sprinkle gelatine into 1/2 cup of the water and let stand for 5 minutes. Pour remaining water into a saucepan with sugar and rinds, simmer gently for 5 minutes. Remove from heat, add gelatine and stir until dissolved. Stir in wine and strain into a bowl. Chill or leave until almost set. Seed grapes if necessary before adding them to the gelee. Turn into pretty stemmed glasses or flutes. *Decorate with sugared grapes.*

Sugared Grapes
  Small bunches of grapes
  1 slightly beaten egg white
  Granulated sugar

Leave grapes in tiny clusters, dab the tops with egg white and roll in the sugar. *These can be used to decorate many desserts.*

BRANDY SNAP CUPS & BANANA CREAM

Preparation time: 30 minutes
Cooking time: 7 minutes
Serves: 8

Chef: Penny Knowles
Yacht: Golden Skye

1/4 cup butter
2 oz. fine sugar
2 Tblsp. golden syrup (no substitute)
2 oz. flour
1/2 tsp. ground ginger
2 tsp. brandy
1 lemon rind, grated

Banana Cream:
  1 cup whipping cream
  Banana liqueur
  2 bananas, thinly sliced

Preheat oven to 350 degrees F.
Melt butter, sugar and syrup. Stir in flour, ginger, brandy and lemon rind. Keep warm until ready to use. On a greased cookie sheet, drop spoonfuls 4 inches apart. Bake for 7 minutes. Cool slightly (1-2 minutes). Lift each cookie with a palette knife and shape over a greased upside down cup. Leave to set. Continue until 8 are made. Whip cream with liqueur.

To serve, place cups on separate small plates, put some cream inside each and decorate with banana slices.

Note: *If the brandy snaps become too hard to mould, return to the oven for 1 minute.*

Hint: *For variation use orange liqueur and orange slices instead of banana. Brandy snaps will keep for several weeks in an airtight container stored in a cool place.*

FABULOUS FRUIT PIZZA

Preparation time: 20 minutes
Cooking time: 10-12 minutes
Chilling time: 1 hour
Serves: 8

Chef: Jan Robinson
Yacht: Vanity

Pizza:
  1 pkg. refrigerator sugar cookie dough
  1 (8 oz.) pkg. cream cheese, softened
  1 cup powdered sugar
  3 Tblsp. lemon juice
  4-5 cups of fruit to cover pizza 1-2 inches high i.e.
    strawberries, blueberries, grapes, bananas,
    kiwifruit, pineapple and peaches
Glaze:
  1 cup orange juice
  1/2 cup lemon juice
  1/2 cup hot water
  3 Tblsp. cornstarch
  1 cup sugar

Preheat oven to 450 degrees F.
Pizza: Slice cookie dough and spread over 12-inch pizza pan to cover pan. Cook as directed on cookie dough package (10-12 minutes in 450 degree oven.) When cooked it will look like one giant golden brown cookie. Mix cream cheese, powdered sugar and lemon juice. Beat until creamy, spread over cookie. Cut up fruit and arrange fruit on top of pizza. Pour cooled glaze over fruit pizza. *Refrigerate and serve when firm and thoroughly cooled.*

Glaze: Cook and stir glaze ingredients until it boils for 30 seconds, then cool.

AMARETTO FREEZE

Preparation time: 10 minutes
Freezing time: 2 hours
Serves: 6

Chef: Jan Robinson
Yacht: Vanity

1/3 cup Amaretto
1 Tblsp. brown sugar
1 quart vanilla ice cream
Whipped cream, optional
Maraschino cherries, optional

Combine Amaretto and sugar, stir until sugar dissolves. Combine ice cream and Amaretto mixture in container of electic blender, process until smooth. Pour into 6 individual freezer-proof serving dishes and freeze. *Just before serving garnish with whipped cream and maraschino cherries.*

FROZEN LEMON SQUARES

Preparation time: 10 minutes
Cooking time: 8 minutes
Freezing time: 4 hours
Serves: 6-9

Chef: Jan Robinson
Yacht: Vanity

1-1/4 cups graham cracker crumbs
1/4 cup sugar
1/4 cup margarine or butter, melted
1 (14 oz.) can sweetened condensed milk
1/2 cup lemon juice
Yellow food coloring, optional
Whipped cream or whipped topping

Preheat oven to 350 degrees F. Combine crumbs, sugar and margarine; press firmly into a 9-inch square pan. In medium bowl, stir milk. lemon juice and coloring. Pour into prepared pan. Bake 8 minutes. Cool. Top with whipped cream. Freeze or chill 4 hours or until firm. *Let stand 10 minutes before serving.*

BROWNIE MINT SUNDAE SQUARES

Preparation time: 10 minutes
Cooking time: about 30 minutes
Freezing time: 6 hours
Serves: 10-12

Chef: Jan Robinson
Yacht: Vanity

1 pkg. fudge brownie mix
1 (14 oz.) can sweetened condensed milk
2 tsp. peppermint extract
Green food coloring (optional)
2 cups whipping cream, whipped
1/2 cup mini-chocolate chips
Hot Fudge Sauce (see recipe below)

Prepare brownie mix as package directs. Turn into greased foil-lined 13x9 inch baking pan. Bake as directed. Cool thoroughly. In a large bowl, combine condensed milk, peppermint and coloring. Fold in whipped cream and chips. Pour over brownie layer. Cover; freeze 6 hours or until firm. *To serve, lift from pan with foil; cut into squares.* Place on individual dessert plates and pass around the *Hot Fudge Sauce.*

Hot Fudge Sauce:
1 (6 oz.) pkg. semi-sweet chocolate chips
2 Tblsp. margarine or butter
1 (14 oz.) can sweetened condensed milk
2 Tblsp. water
1 tsp. vanilla extract

In heavy saucepan, over medium heat, cook together the first four ingredients, stir constantly until thickened, about 5 minutes. Add vanilla and serve in a pitcher.

Notes

FRUIT AND FRUIT DESSERTS

Notes

ALLIGATOR SWEET MEAT

Preparation time: 5 days
Cooking time: 2 days
Serves: 982

Chef: Suzan Salisbury
Yacht: Gypsy

20 lbs. butter
30 lbs. brown sugar
10 lbs. cinnamon
90 ripe bananas
1 medium size Florida alligator, skinned
4 boxes raisins
4 cases Cruzan rum
15 gal. vanilla ice cream
Garnish: Fresh green lily pads

Build a fire, ready to use when flames are medium high. Melt butter in a very large skillet (stainless steel water tank is about the right size). Add brown sugar and cinnamon. Heat until bubbly, stirring constantly. Add chopped bananas and saute until bananas are soft. Add whole alligator to skillet and cook over medium high fire until browned on both sides. Remove 'Gator and set aside. Add raisins to skillet and warm.

Meanwhile, using a West Indian machete, cut 'Gator into bite size chunks. After 'Gator is cut up, return pieces to skillet with sauce. Add rum and reheat. Remove from heat and ignite. Baste 'Gator until flames die. *Serve on top of fresh green lily pads with vanilla ice cream; accompany with fresh minty frog legs.*

Get him honey this recipe calls for it!

APPLE–WALNUT SQUARES

Preparation time: 25 minutes   *Chef: Jan Robinson*
Cooking time: 40 minutes   *Yacht: Vanity*
Makes: 2 dozen

2 cups all-purpose flour
2 cups brown sugar, firmly packed
1/2 cup butter, softened
1 cup walnuts, chopped
1 tsp. cinnamon
1 tsp. baking soda
1/4 tsp. salt
1 egg
1 cup sour cream
1 tsp. vanilla
2 large apples, peeled, cored and finely chopped
Garnish: vanilla ice cream

Preheat oven to 350 degrees F.
Lightly grease 9x13-inch baking dish. Combine first 3
ingredients in medium bowl and mix until finely crumbled.
Stir in nuts. Press 2 cups of mixture evenly into bottom of
prepared dish. Add cinnamon, baking soda, and salt to
remaining mixture and blend well. Beat in egg, sour cream,
and vanilla. Gently stir in apples. Spoon evenly into dish.
Bake until cake begins to pull away from sides of dish and
tester inserted in center comes out clean, about 35 to 40
minutes. Let cool completely in pan. Cut into squares.

Serve topped with vanilla ice cream.

BAKED APPLE DUMPLINGS

Preparation time: 20 minutes   *Chef: Paulette Hadley*
Cooking time: 30-40 minutes   *Yacht: Chardonnay*
Serves: 4-10

1/2 recipe Flaky Pastry (see below)
6 medium-size tart cooking apples, peeled and cored
2 cups water
1-1/2 cups sugar
1/4 cup butter or margarine
1-3/4 tsp. ground cinnamon
Garnish: cream or whipped cream

Preheat oven to 425 degrees F.
In a saucepan bring water, 1 cup sugar, 3 Tblsp. butter and 1/4 teaspoon cinnamon to a boil. Roll pastry out to 1/8 inch plus thickness, cut into six 7 inch squares. Place apples on squares. Mix remaining sugar and cinnamon, fill apple cavities, dot with remaining butter. Bring opposite points of pastry up over apple, overlap, moisten and seal. Lift carefully, place a few inches apart in baking dish. Pour hot syrup around dumplings. Bake until crust is well browned and apples are tender. *Serve warm with cream or whipped cream.*

Flaky Pastry (For two 9-inch pie crusts)
   4 cups all-purpose flour
   1-3/4 cups vegetable shortening or lard (not oil)
   1 tsp. sugar
   2 tsp. salt
   1/2 cup water
   1 Tblsp. vinegar
   1 egg

In a large bowl, mix first 4 ingredients with a fork. In a small bowl beat water and remaining ingredients together. Add to first mix, blend with fork until dry ingredients are moistened. Hand mold dough into a ball, chill 15 minutes.

Note: *Refrigerated dough lasts up to 3 days, or freeze until ready to use. Refrigerated dough can be rolled at once.*

CARIBBEAN APPLE FLAMBE

Preparation time: 20 minutes   *Chef: Gabrielle Rapp*
Cooking time: 40 minutes   *Yacht: Vanita*
Serves: 4

4 apples, medium size
1 cup raisins
1/2 cup nuts (preferably almonds)
4 tsp. sugar
4 tsp. honey
1 tsp. cinnamon
1/2 cup dark rum
Calvados (apple brandy)
Garnish: whipped cream and cinnamon

Preheat oven to 350 degrees F.
In a saucepan mix raisins, nuts, sugar, honey, cinnamon and rum, simmer about 10 minutes or until the rum has soaked into the raisins. Meanwhile, wash, dry and core apples, plug the bottom of the hollows with aluminum foil (remove when baked). Fill apple centers with raisin mixture.

Place on a baking sheet or aluminum foil and bake for 30 minutes. When done (apples should be soft to poke but skin not broken) remove and place on a warm serving platter. Pour over a generous swig of Calvados and flambe! *Serve with whipped cream and a sprinkle of cinnamon.*

Note: *Apples must be served immediately after they come out of the oven, otherwise they shrivel up.*

For a change of pace, try the following fillings: fresh raspberries and Himbeergeist (raspberry schnapps),or plum jam and Slibonite (plum schnapps). Great for the digestion!

BACON WRAPPED BANANAS

Preparation time: 5 minutes
Cooking time: 10 minutes
Serves: 6

Chef: Sharon Davis
Yacht: Quê Sera

6 bananas
6 slices bacon
1 Tblsp. butter
1/2 tsp. cinnamon
2 oz. rum
Garnish: whipped cream and grated nutmeg

Peel bananas and slice in half lengthwise. Cut bacon slices in half. Wrap bacon around banana, secure with a toothpick. In a frying pan, melt butter and add bananas, fry over medium heat until bacon is done, turning to cook on each side. Sprinkle with cinnamon, add rum and cook 2-3 minutes more. *Serve this treat with your favorite coffee.*

CARIBBEAN BANANAS

Preparation time: 15 minutes
Cooking time: 15 minutes
Serves: 4-6

Chef: Peggy Curren
Yacht: Traveline

1/4 cup margarine or butter
4 medium bananas, peeled
1/3 cup packed brown sugar
1 Tblsp. lemon juice
1/2 tsp ground allspice
1/4 cup light rum

Preheat oven to 350 degrees F.
Coat bottom of baking dish with margarine. Cut bananas in half lengthwise and in half crosswise, making 4 pieces. Place cut sides down in a baking dish. Mix brown sugar, lemon juice and allspice, drizzle over bananas and bake uncovered for 15 minutes. *To serve, heat rum until warm, ignite and pour over bananas.*

BROILED BANANAS

Preparation time: 15 minutes   *Chef: John Freeman*
Cooking time: 5 minutes   *Yacht: Solid Gold, Too*
Chilling time: 10 minutes
Serves: 6

5 large bananas, peeled
1/4 tsp. cinnamon
1/4 tsp. ground cloves
1/4 tsp. dried lemon peel
1/4 cup raisins
Juice and zest of 1 lemon
6 oranges, peeled and segmented
6 tsp. Creme de Banana liqueur
2 Tblsp. brown sugar
3 Tblsp. butter

Cut bananas into half inch pieces. Mix together cinnamon, cloves, lemon peel, raisins, lemon juice and zest. Lightly mix bananas into mixture. Distribute banana mixture evenly among 6 ramekin dishes. Top with orange segments. Add one teaspoon of liqueur to each dish and sprinkle brown sugar on top. Chill for 10 minutes. Top each with a pat of butter and broil 5 minutes or until caramelized.

_ *I wouldn't go for this recipe,
you'll get creamed man!*

CARIBBEAN BANANA FLAMBE'

Preparation time: 10 minutes   *Chef: Marilyn Stenberg*
Cooking time: 5 minutes   *Yacht: Sabina D*
Serves: 4

1 Tblsp. white sesame seeds
3 Tblsp. shredded coconut
4 firm under-ripe bananas
2 Tblsp. unsalted butter
1 Tblsp. finely minced ginger
2 tsp. grated orange peel
2 Tblsp. sugar
Juice of one lime
6 Tblsp. rum
Garnish: Lime wedges

Toast sesame seeds in an ungreased skillet until light golden, set aside. Repeat with coconut. Peel bananas, cut in half lengthwise, place in skillet over medium heat, add butter, ginger and orange peel. When bubbling add bananas, cut side down. Sprinkle with sugar and lime juice, saute for 1 minute. Carefully turn over and saute until sauce begins to caramelize, about 1 minute. Transfer bananas to warm dessert plates. Sprinkle with coconut and sesame seeds. Return pan to meduim heat, add the rum, when hot ignite with a match. Immediately pour sauce over bananas. *Serve at once with lime wedges.*

These bananas are excellent served with ginger or coconut ice cream. You can also flambe' with cognac instead of rum and garnish with brandy snaps.

AMARETTO YOGURT PARFAIT

Preparation time: 10 minutes   *Chef: Karen Ciminelli*
Marinating time: 8 hours   *Yacht: Annie Laurie*
Serves: 6-8

Fresh fruit (apples, pears, strawberries, etc.)
3 (8 oz.) cartons of your favorite yogurt
Amaretto, or liqueur of your choice
Garnish: whipped cream and shortbread cookies

Cut up fruit and marinate in Amaretto all day. In a parfait glass: layer fruit, yogurt and Amaretto until full. *Top with whipped cream and cookie.*

SOUTH SEA BANANAS

Preparation time: 10 minutes   *Chef: Jan Robinson*
Cooking time: 20 minutes   *Yacht: Vanity*
Serves: 4

4 bananas, peeled and sliced lengthwise
1/2 cup brown sugar
1 tsp. cinnamon
2 Tblsp. butter
1/4 cup orange juice
1/2 cup shredded coconut
Garnish: orange slices

Preheat oven to 350 degrees F.
Arrange bananas in a well greased oven dish. Mix the sugar and cinnamon together. Sprinkle over the bananas. Cut the butter into small pieces, and scatter over bananas. Carefully pour the orange juice and sprinkle the top with the coconut. Place in oven and cook for about 20 minutes, or until coconut is browned and the fruit is soft. Garnish with orange slices. *Serve hot.*

BRANDY COMPOTE

Preparation time: 15 minutes
Cooking time: 10 minutes
Serves: 6

Chef: Wendy Smith
Yacht: Hiya

4 Tblsp. butter
3 Tblsp. sugar
1/3 cup orange marmalade
1 jar apricot baby food
2 Tblsp. lemon juice
2 apples, unpeeled, cored and chopped
1 Tblsp. currants or raisins
1/3 cup sliced almonds
1/4 cup warm brandy
1 cup heavy cream, whipped
1 pound cake, sliced
Garnish: sliced almonds

Melt the butter in a saucepan and mix in the sugar. Add the marmalade, apricot and lemon juice, heat well. Add fruits and nuts just before serving. To serve place a pound cake slice on each plate, ladle compote over the cake then flambe with warm brandy. Pass around unsweetened whipped cream. *Garnish with sliced almonds.*

FRUIT COMPOTE

Preparation time: 15 minutes
Cooking time: 3-5 minutes
Serves: 6

Chef: Jan Robinson
Yacht: Vanity

2 bananas
2 slices pineapple
1 small bunch grapes
2 oranges
Grated coconut, optional
4 Tblsp. butter
1 tsp. cinnamon
Dash vanilla
2-3 Tblsp. favorite liqueur

Chop any combination of fruit you have and saute in butter until everything is coated. Add bananas last as they cook fast. Add rest of ingredients. Flambe with your favorite liqueur. *Serve warm with your choice of cream or ice cream.*

Note: *To cut calories, saute fruit in lite butter or a butter substitute and serve with coffee -* **no** *cream or ice cream.*

CARIBBEAN FRUIT BOWL

Preparation time: 15 minutes   *Chef: Sande Buxton*
Cooking time: none   *Yacht: Ambience*
Serves: 4

1 mango, peeled and thinly sliced
2 cups raspberries
6 fresh apricots
2 Tblsp. sugar
Juice of 1 orange
2 Tblsp. light rum
Garnish: whipped cream

Remove stones from apricots and slice thinly. Place in a bowl with mango and raspberries, sprinkle with sugar and toss. Add orange juice and rum, toss gently. Let marinate 15 minutes, or until ready to serve. *Serve in separate bowls with whipped cream. This is an easy pleaser.*

FRUITY FINALE

Preparation time: 25 minutes   *Chef: Suzan Salisbury*
Chilling time: 1 hour   *Yacht: Gypsy*
Serves: 6

2 (11 oz.) cans Mandarin oranges
1-1/2 cups melon balls
2 bananas, peeled and sliced
1/2 cup seedless green grapes
2 Tblsp. lemon juice
1 tsp. almond extract
1 Tblsp. Grand Marnier
Garnish: shredded coconut, slice of kiwifruit or parsley

Put drained oranges in a bowl with melon, bananas, grapes, lemon juice, almond extract and Grand Marnier. Toss gently. Chill for 1 hour. Divide into 6 dessert dishes. *Top with coconut, garnish and serve.*

CHERRIES JUBILEE

Preparation time: 5 minutes   *Chef: Paulette Hadley*
Cooking time: 2 minutes   *Yacht: Chardonnay*
Serves: 6

1 Tblsp. sugar
2 Tblsp. cornstarch
2 cups pitted black cherries, drained (save juice)
1 tsp. grated orange rind
1/3 cup fruit brandy (e.g. cherry, peach...)
1 Tblsp. Cognac
Vanilla ice cream

Mix sugar and cornstarch. Gradually add cherry juice while cooking over direct heat, stirring constantly until thickened and clear. Add cherries, grated orange rind, and brandy. Place over filled hot water pan. Heat 1 tablespoon cognac over another heat source and pour into ladle, ignite and pour over cherry mixture. When flames subside, ladle over vanilla ice cream in individual serving dishes.

Elegant, but very easy.

CURRIED FRUIT BAKE

Preparation time: 10 minutes　　　　*Chef: Jan Robinson*
Cooking time: 10 minutes　　　　　　*Yacht: Vanity*
Serves: 4-6

4 cups fruit, peaches, pears, pineapple, canned
1/4 cup red wine
3 Tblsp. brown sugar
2 tsp. curry powder
Garnish: sour cream, yogurt or ice cream and
　　vanilla cookie crumbs (optional)

In a saucepan over low heat, gently warm the fruit in wine.
Add brown sugar and sprinkle with curry, mix well. *Serve
in individual dishes and top each portion with ice cream,
sour cream or yogurt, then sprinkle with vanilla cookie
crumbs.*

Note:*To cut calories, saute fruit in light butter or a butter
substitute and serve with coffee -* **no** *cream or ice cream, or
cookie crumbs.*

FRUIT SALAD WITH SHERRY

Preparation time: 15 minutes   *Chef: Jan Robinson*
Chilling time: 1 hour   *Yacht: Vanity*
Serves: 4

2 medium oranges, peeled
2 bananas, peeled
1 apple, peeled and cored
1 pear, peeled and cored
1/2 cup sherry
2 kiwi fruit
1 honey-dew melon or 1/2 small watermelon,
** scooped into balls**
2 passionfruit (if available)
Honey to taste

Cube oranges, apple and pear, scoop out passionfruit, slice bananas; add melon balls, and honey. Pour sherry over and mix lightly. *Chill for 1 hour before serving. Garnish with mint leaves.*

This is a wonderful potpourri of fresh fruits to provide vitamins and minerals. Honey is used as a natural sweetening and for it's flavor.

GINGERED PEARS

Preparation time: 10 minutes   *Chef: Jan Robinson*
Cooking time: 10 minutes (microwave)   *Yacht: Vanity*
Serves: 6

3 pears, peeled
1 Tblsp. butter or margarine
2 Tblsp. honey
1/2 tsp. ground ginger
3 Tblsp. light rum
1/4 cup almonds, sliced
Vanilla ice cream

Cut pears in half lengthwise and seed. Place pears, cut side down, in a 2 quart, shallow casserole dish and set aside. Place butter in a 1 cup glass measure, microwave on high for 35 seconds or until melted. Add honey, ginger and rum, stir well. Pour over pears. Cover tightly with heavy-duty plastic wrap, fold back a corner of wrap to allow steam to escape. Microwave on high 4 to 6 minutes or until pears are done. Spread almonds in a glass pie plate, microwave on high 4 to 5 minutes or until toasted.

To serve: place a pear half in each individual serving dish, place a scoop of ice cream on top of pears. Drizzle with pear sauce and sprinkle with almonds.

EASY GRAPEFRUIT DESSERT

Preparation time: 5 minutes   *Chef: Jan Robinson*
Cooking time: 1 minute   *Yacht: Vanity*
Serves: 6

3 grapefruits, cut in half
2 Tblsp. apricot preserves
1 Tblsp. rum
Sprinkle of allspice or nutmeg
Garnish: halved pecans

Section and remove seeds from the halved grapefruits. Mix apricot preserves with the rum and spread over grapefruit. Sprinkle with nutmeg or allspice and put under broiler for a minute, watch carefully. *Put a pecan half in the center of each and serve.*

GO-MANGO

Preparation time: 15 minutes   *Chef: Ninia Cunningham*
Cooking time: none   *Yacht: Iona of the Islands*
Serves: 4

4 large, very ripe mangoes
Juice of 1/2 lemon
3-4 oz. confectioners sugar
1-1/2 cups whipping cream

Peel mangoes and remove the flesh from stone. Blend into a smooth puree. Stir in lemon juice and most of the sugar. Add remaining sugar to taste if fruit is not sweet enough. Whip the cream. In tall glasses layer the puree and whipped cream for effect, make the last layer whipped cream. Decorate with pieces of mango. Or, whipped cream can be folded into the puree and served as a mousse.

MANGO FLAMBE

Preparation time: 5 minutes
Cooking time: 5 minutes
Serves: 4

Chef: Amanda Baker
Yacht: Gypsy Wind

4 medium mangoes
Brown sugar
Butter
Cinnamon
Apricot brandy
Garnish: 4 small bunches of black grapes

Peel mangoes carefully, then cut the meat off the stone in pieces as big as possible. Melt butter, brown sugar and cinnamon in a saucepan. Very quickly saute fruit until glazed. Pour on apricot brandy and flambe. *Serve immediately while flaming with a little of the sauce. Garnish with a small bunch of grapes on each plate - makes this dish look very appetizing!*

PEACH BRULEE

Preparation time: 20 minutes
Cooking time: 8-10 minutes
Chilling time: 30 minutes
Serves: 6

Chef: Penny Knowles
Yacht: Golden Skye

6 peach halves (canned)
1 tsp. cinnamon
1/4 cup of brown sugar
2 cups sour cream
1/2 cup white sugar

Place peach halves in six ramekins, sprinkle with cinnamon and brown sugar. Cover with sour cream and top evenly with white sugar. Place under broiler close to heat and broil until sugar is melted and caramelized, about 5 minutes. *Let cool and chill before serving.*

TOXICATED PEACHES

Preparation time: 10 minutes
Serves: 6

Chef: Karen Roest
Yacht: Rising Sun 64

6 Tblsp. Courvoisier
1 large can halved peaches
Whipped cream
Cinnamon
Garnish: cherries

In six dessert bowls place 1 tablespoon Courvoisier. Place a peach half in each bowl with hollow side up. Cover generously with the juice from the can. Place whipped cream over peach half and sprinkle with cinnamon, place a cherry on top and serve.

Hint: *If whipped cream is unavailable, simply sprinkle cinnamon over peach and put a cherry in the hollow.*

LOVE BITE PRUNES AND APRICOTS

Preparation time: 5 minutes
Chilling time: overnight
Serves: 4

Chef: Jan Robinson
Yacht: Vanity

1-1/4 cups dried apricots
1-1/4 cups dried prunes
1 Tblsp. raisins
1 Tblsp. fresh lemon, chopped
1 orange peel
Boiling water
1 Tblsp. honey
2 cloves (if desired)
1 Tblsp. lemon juice
Garnish: plain yogurt

Wash dried fruit, lemon and orange peel and place in a dish, pour over enough boiling water to cover, add honey and stir until dissolved. Add cloves and lemon juice. Chill overnight. *Before serving, remove cloves. Good with plain yogurt.*

A nice tangy dessert, or great for breakfast with granola.

POACHED PEARS IN CHAMPAGNE

Preparation time: 10 minutes   *Chef: Ninia Cunningham*
Cooking time: 50 minutes   *Yacht: Iona of the Islands*
Serves: 6

6 firm Anjou pears
3/4 cup sugar
1-1/2 cups champagne or white wine
1/2 cup water
1 cinnamon stick
Pared rind of 1/2 lemon or lime
Juice of 1/2 lemon or lime

Gently bring last 6 ingredients to boil in a saucepan large enough to hold the 6 pears standing up. Cut a slice from the base of each pear, then peel them leaving the stalk on. Place upright in the pan with poaching liquid, simmer gently 40 minutes or until pears are tender when pierced with a sharp knife. Remove pears with a slotted spoon. Place in serving dishes. Reduce remaining liquid until it forms a syrup, pour a little syrup over each pear.

Variation 1: Use red wine instead of champagne.

Variation 2: *Chocaholic Pears (see page 175).*

CHOCAHOLIC PEARS

Preparation time: 10 minutes   *Chef: Ninia Cunningham*
Cooking time: 40 minutes   *Yacht: Iona of the Islands*
Serves: 6

6 firm Anjou pears
4 oz. semi-sweet chocolate
2 Tblsp. strong instant coffee
2 Tblsp. butter
1 Tblsp. rum
2 eggs, separated
Garnish: Whipped cream

Poach the pears as directed in **Poached Pears in Champagne** (see page 174). Remove pears with slotted spoon, reserving liquid for next batch or for **Wine Gelee** (see page 147). Chill pears. Make chocolate glaze as follows. Melt chocolate in a double boiler or bowl set over a pan of boiling water, stir occasionally. Remove from heat. Beat in butter, egg yolks and rum. In a separate bowl beat egg whites; not too stiffly. Fold into chocolate mixture with a spoon. Coat pears evenly. *Serve with whipped cream.*

Chef Bill Horne on Yacht Ambience, suggests you combine the following ingredients for his **Chocolate Pears**

4 oz. semi-sweet chocolate
1-1/2 cups powdered sugar
3 Tblsp. heavy cream
1 Tblsp. white rum
Garnish: 1/4 cup slivered almonds

In a double boiler, melt the above ingredients over medium-low heat, stirring constantly. When thickened, remove and let cool. Spoon chocolate over pears and sprinkle with almonds. Refrigerate to set the chocolate before serving.

GLAZED PINEAPPLE SLICES

Preparation time: 10 minutes　　　　*Chef: Jan Robinson*
Cooking time: 10 minutes　　　　　　*Yacht: Vanity*
Serves: 4

1 Fresh pineapple, or 6 to 8 canned slices
1/2 cup sugar
1/2 cup water
2 Tblsp. white vinegar
3 or 4 pieces crystallized ginger
Garnish: whipped cream

Cut the pineapple in 6 or 8 half inch slices, reserving any syrup that forms during cutting. Put this syrup, together with the sugar, water, and vinegar into a saucepan. Finely chop or crush the ginger, and add to the mixture. Bring to a boil and simmer for about 5 minutes. Add the pineapple slices, and continue simmering until they are clear and have absorbed most of the syrup. *Serve cold with or without cream for dessert.*

Note: *Also good served hot with pork, ham or chicken.*

RASPBERRY FOOL

Preparation time: 10 minutes　　　*Chef: Jan Robinson*
Cooking time: none　　　　　　　*Yacht:Vanity*
Serves: 4

**1 (10 oz.) pkg. frozen quick-thaw raspberries
in light syrup, thawed
1 cup heavy or whipping cream
1/8 tsp. almond extract
Garnish: mint leaves**

Begin recipe about 20 minutes before serving. Over a medium bowl, press raspberries through a sieve; discard seeds. In a small bowl, with mixer at medium speed, beat cream and almond extract until soft peaks form. With rubber spatula or wire whisk, fold whipped cream into raspberry puree. Spoon raspberry mixture into 4 parfait glasses or dessert dishes. *Garnish with mint leaves.*

STRAWBERRIES SNOW WHITE

Preparation time: 30 minutes　　　*Chef: Fiona Dugdale*
Cooking time: none　　　　　　　*Yacht: Promenade*
Serves: 8

**4 pints strawberries
2 cups heavy cream
1 Tblsp. sugar
3 Tblsp. Grand Marnier
2 oranges
2 bananas (optional)
2 kiwifruit**

Clean and hull strawberries, chill. Whip together cream, sugar and Grand Marnier until stiff, do not over whip. Grate orange peel. Peel and slice oranges, bananas, and kiwifruit. Spread cream mixture evenly on dessert plates. Arrange sliced fruit and sprinkle grated orange rind. Dot each one with 7 strawberries, pointed end up. *Enjoy!*

Notes

PIES

Notes

APPLE BERRY COBBLER

Preparation time: 30 minutes
Cooking time: 45 minutes
Serves: 6 or more

Chef: Beth Avore
Yacht: Perfection

**1 (16oz) can apple pie filling or 6 apples
(cored, peeled and sliced)**
**1 (16oz) can berry pie filling or 2 cups
fresh or frozen berries, any type will do**
1/2-3/4 cup sugar
1 cup flour
1-1/2 cups oatmeal
1 tsp. cinnamon
Dash nutmeg
Dash ground cloves
1/2 cup (4 oz.) butter
**Garnish: *apple skin rose or design of berries
and apple slices and ice cream, fresh cream,
or Cool Whip (optional)**

Preheat oven to 350 degrees F.
In a 2 quart casserole dish mix cans of fruit together (for fresh fruit dot with butter and sprinkle with 1/2-3/4 cup of sugar and season to taste.) In a mixing bowl start with flour and mix in oatmeal, sugar, cinnamon, nutmeg and cloves. Cut butter into mixture with hands. The batter should be crumbly, but sticky enough to hold together if lightly squeezed. Add more butter if necessary. Sprinkle over the top of fruit to cover but do not pack tightly. *This is good served plain, but also tasty with fresh cream, Cool Whip or ice cream. Best when served warm.*

Hint: **To make an apple skin rose; with a paring knife start at the blossom end of apple and skin the fruit in a 3/4" strip of one piece, be careful not to break. Start at the same end and coil the peel around itself tightly to form "bud" then looser to form "petals". Arrange in center of dish and bake.*

PEACH COBBLER

Preparation time: 20 minutes
Cooking time: 25-30 minutes
Serves: 6-8

Chef: Paulette Hadley
Yacht: Chardonnay

Filling:
- 1/4 cup butter
- 1 cup sugar
- 1 Tblsp. cornstarch
- 1/2 tsp. cinnamon
- 1/4 tsp. allspice
- 3/4 cup water
- 1/4 cup sherry
- 6-8 fresh peaches
- 2 Tblsp. lemon juice
- 1/4 cup pecans, coarsley chopped

Dough:
- 1/4 cup sugar
- 2 cups packaged biscuit mix
- 1 egg, slightly beaten
- 1/2 cup milk
- 1/2 tsp. almond extract

Preheat oven to 375 degrees F.

Filling: In the oven, melt butter in an oblong 2 quart baking dish. In a saucepan, combine the next six filling ingredients and boil for one minute. Skin and half peaches and arrange in the baking dish. Pour hot mixture over peaches and sprinkle with lemon juice and pecans.

Dough: Mix together dough ingredients and spoon around the edge of the filling. Bake for 25-30 minutes. *Serve warm.*

EASY COBBLER

Preparation time: 5 minutes   *Chef: Candice Carson*
Cooking time: 25 minutes   *Yacht: Freight Train II*
Serves: 6

1 (16 oz.) can pie filling (cherry, blueberry, etc.)
1/2 box white cake mix
1/4 cup butter
1/2 cup nuts
Garnish: whipped cream

Preheat oven to 350 degrees F.
Spread pie filling in an 8 inch square pan. Sprinkle the white cake mix on the pie filling, dab with pats of butter and sprinkle nuts on top. Bake until golden brown. *I usually serve this hot in pretty glass bowls topped with whipped cream.*

MAPLE APPLE CRISP

Preparation time: 10 minutes   *Chef: Peggy Curren*
Cooking time: 35 minutes   *Yacht: Traveline*
Serves: 6-8

5-6 apples, peeled, cored and sliced
3/4 cup maple syrup
1/2 cup all-purpose flour
1/2 cup rolled oats
1/2 cup brown sugar
1/2 cup butter
Salt

Preheat oven to 375 degrees F.
Place apple slices in an 8 inch square baking dish. Pour maple syrup over apples. Combine remaining ingredients and mix until texture resembles bread crumbs. Sprinkle this mixture over apples and bake for about 35 minutes.

Wonderful when served with vanilla ice cream on top.

PEAR CRANBERRY CRISP

Preparation time: 10 minutes   *Chef: Jean Crook*
Cooking time: 3 minutes (microwave)   *Yacht: Dileas*
Serves: 4

2 pears
1 cup cranberries
1/3 cup rolled oats
1/3 cup 100% Bran or All Bran cereal
1/3 cup brown sugar, packed
1/4 tsp. cinnamon
2 Tblsp. butter

Peel, core and slice pears, toss with cranberries in a 6 cup microwavable baking dish. Combine rolled oats, bran cereal, brown sugar and cinnamon. With a pastry blender cut in the butter, breaking up bran cereal slightly. Sprinkle over fruit. Microwave uncovered on high for 3 minutes or until fruit is tender.

SUPER CRISP

Preparation time: 15 minutes   *Chef: Suzan Salisbury*
Cooking time: 20 minutes   *Yacht: Gypsy*
Serves: 8

1 cup all-purpose flour
1 cup rolled oats
1 cup brown sugar
1/2 cup butter
2 cans apple pie filling
1 tsp. cinnamon
Garnish: red cherries, pitted and halved

Preheat oven to 350 degrees F.
Mix flour, oats, sugar and butter until crumbly. Put pie filling in a greased 8x8-inch baking dish and sprinkle with cinnamon. Sprinkle flour mixture over pie filling, bake until filling starts to bubble through the topping.

To serve: Garnish with the cherries and/or accompany with vanilla ice cream for Mom's favorite. Serve warm.

The directions on frozen pies say to cut slits in top crust, but it is difficult when solid frozen. After the pie has been in hot oven for a few minutes, it will be soft enough to open up at the drop of a knife point.

PEAR CHEDDAR CRUMBLE

Preparation time: 10 minutes
Cooking time: 45-50 minutes
Serves: 6

Chef: Jean Crook
Yacht: Dileas

1/2 cup all-purpose flour
1/2 cup cheddar cheese, shredded
1/3 cup walnuts
1/3 cup brown sugar
1 tsp. cinnamon
1/3 cup cold unsalted butter
5 pears peeled, cored, halved and sliced

Preheat oven to 350 degrees F.
Combine flour, cheese, walnuts, sugar and cinnamon.
With a pastry blender or two knives cut in butter until
mixture resembles course crumbs. Arrange pears in buttered
8 inch square baking dish. Sprinkle with crumb mixture
and bake for 45-50 minutes or until pears are tender. *Serve
warm or cold.*

Hint: *If pears are not very ripe, increase the brown sugar
to 2/3 cup.*

APPLE CHEESECAKE TART

Preparation time: 20 minutes　　　　*Chef: Allison Moir*
Cooking time: 35 minutes　　　　*Yacht: Pride of Lyn*
Serves: 8-10

Crust:
  1/2 cup butter
  1/3 cup sugar
  1/4 tsp. vanilla
  1 cup flour
Filling:
  1 (8 oz.) pkg. cream cheese
  1/2 tsp. vanilla
  1 egg
  1/4 cup sugar
Topping:
  3-4 apples, peeled, cored and sliced
  1/3 cup sugar
  3/4 tsp. cinnamon
  1/2 cup almonds, sliced
Garnish: whipped cream and almonds

Preheat oven to 425 degrees F.
Crust: Cream butter, sugar and vanilla. Add flour and blend. In a 9-inch torte or springform pan, spread dough evenly on bottom and 1 inch up sides.

Filling: Blend together cream cheese, vanilla, egg and sugar until smooth and pour into crust.

Topping: Fold together all ingredients and place over filling in a C-shaped pattern. Sprinkle almonds on top, bake 10 minutes, then reduce heat to 400 degrees F. and bake 25 minutes.

Serve garnished with piped whipped cream or add a dollop to each serving, sprinkle almonds on top. Yum, Yum!!

APPLE CRUMB PIE

Preparation time: 20 minutes   *Chef: Judy Knape*
Cooking time: 50 minutes   *Yacht: Endless Summer 48*
Serves: 6-8

4 or 5 large tart apples
1/2 cup granulated sugar
1 tsp. cinnamon
9-inch pie shell, uncooked
1 tsp. lemon juice
1/2 cup brown sugar
3/4 cup flour
1/3 cup margarine
Garnish: whipped cream or ice cream

Preheat oven to 400 degrees F.
Peel, core and slice apples. Mix granulated sugar and cinnamon. Sprinkle over apples and put mixture in pie shell. Sprinkle with lemon juice. Sift together brown sugar and flour, cut in margarine until crumbly and put on apples. Bake 40-50 minutes.

Slice and serve with a dollop of whipped cream or ice cream.

BERNARD'S APPLE PIE

Preparation time: 30 minutes   *Chef: Kelly Reed*
Cooking time: 65 minutes   *Yacht: Capricious*
Serves: 8

9-inch pie crust, uncooked
Filling:
  5-8 Granny Smith apples, peeled, cored and sliced
  1 cup sour cream
  1 cup sugar
  1/3 cup all-purpose flour
  1 egg
  2 tsp. vanilla
  1/2 tsp. salt
Topping:
  1 cup walnuts or pecans, chopped
  1/2 cup all-purpose flour
  1/3 cup firmly packed brown sugar
  1/3 cup granulated sugar
  Pinch of salt
  1 Tblsp. cinnamon
  1/2 cup butter, softened
Garnish: vanilla ice cream

Preheat oven to 450 degrees F.
Filling: Mix all ingredients well. Spoon into uncooked pie crust, bake for 10 minutes, reduce heat to 350 degrees F. and bake 40 minutes (crust may need a foil shield).

Topping: Combine ingredients and mix well. Spoon over pie and bake 15 minutes longer at 350 degrees F. *Serve with vanilla ice cream on top.*

This is everybody's favorite!

CHILLED BANANA–MANGO CREAM PIE

Preparation time: 10 minutes　　　*Chef: John Freeman*
Chilling time: 2 hours　　　　　　*Yacht: Solid Gold, Too*
Serves: 10

Crust:
  1 lb. granola
  2 Tblsp. raisins
  2 Tblsp. light brown sugar
  4 Tblsp. butter, melted
Filling:
  1 (8 oz.) pkg. cream cheese
  1/4 cup powdered sugar
  Lemon juice
  1/2 tsp. dried orange peel
  2 Tblsp. Creme de Banana liqueur
  2 Tblsp. light rum
  1/2 tsp. cinnamon
  1-1/2 cups ripe bananas, pureed
  1 cup heavy cream or whipping cream
  1 pkg. plain gelatin, dissolved in 3 Tblsp. water
Garnish: mango puree

Crust: Mix all crust ingredients together in a food processor. Blend for approximately 15 seconds. Press into the bottom of a 9-inch springform pan.

Filling: In a blender mix together cream cheese, sugar and lemon juice, blend until smooth. Add orange peel, liqueur, rum, cinnamon and pureed bananas, mix well. Add cream, mix lightly. Add dissolved gelatin, mix until smooth. Pour into pan and refrigerate for one hour.

Top with mango puree and refrigerate for at least one more hour.

ZINFANDEL PEAR TART

Preparation time: 30 minutes   *Chef: Aija Eglite*
Cooking time: 20 minutes   *Yacht: Rhapsody*
Clilling time: overnight
Serves: 8

2 cups white Zinfandel wine
1/2 cup sugar
1 whole vanilla bean
2 strips orange peel
2 strips lemon peel
5 pears, Bosc if possible; peeled, cored, and halved,
5 apples, Rome Beauty if possible; peeled,
   cored and sliced.
2 Tblsp. butter
1 Tblsp. water
1 cinnamon stick
1/2 tsp. ground cloves
10-inch baked tart shell

Prepare fruit a day ahead of time. Combine wine, sugar, vanilla bean, and citrus peels, simmer 5 minutes. Add pears and simmer 15-20 minutes, chill in liquid overnight. Combine apples, butter, water, cinnamon and cloves. In a saucepan, cook over medium-low heat until apples are soft, chill overnight. Spread the apple sauce evenly in tart shell. Drain pears, reserving 1 cup of liquid, slice and arrange over apples. Cook reserved poaching liquid over high heat to reduce and thicken.

When serving, spoon a small amount of sauce over tart slices.

CIA STRAWBERRY GOAT CHEESE TART

Preparation time: 15 minutes *Chef: Candice Carson*
Cooking time: 20 minutes   *Yacht: Freight Train II*
Serves: 6-8

1-1/4 cups soft goat cheese
1/3 cup sugar
1 Tblsp. flour
2 eggs
9-inch pie shell, baked
1 pint strawberries, cut in half
1/2 cup glaze
Garnish: whipped cream

Preheat oven to 350 degrees F.
Cream the cheese, butter and sugar until smooth. Add flour and mix in eggs one at a time, scrape bowl after each addition. Fill pie shell and bake until cheese filling is firm (about 20 minutes), cool. Arrange strawberries on top, cut side up, points inward. Spoon glaze over the top and chill. *Garnish with whipped cream.*

Before baking all filled pies or tarts, place rack in lower third of oven for more even heating.

BROWNIE FUDGE PIE

Preparation time: 30 minutes   *Chef: Liz Thomas-Gibson*
Cooking time: 30-35 minutes   *Yacht: Tranquility*
Chilling time: 4 hours or more
Serves: 8-10

1/4 cup butter
3/4 cup brown sugar, packed
1 (12 oz.) pkg. semi-sweet chocolate morsels
3 eggs, beaten
1/4 cup flour
1 cup walnut or pecans, coarsely chopped
1 tsp. vanilla
9-inch pie shell, uncooked
Garnish: whipped cream or ice cream

Preheat oven to 375 degrees F.
In a saucepan melt butter, brown sugar and chocolate morsels together. Cool. Add eggs. Combine flour and nuts, add to chocolate mixture. Stir in vanilla. Pour into a pie shell and bake for 30-35 minutes. Cool and refrigerate for 4 hours or more. *Serve topped with whipped cream or ice cream.*

Kids love this pie, it is very rich. I have a hard time keeping ice cream, but this pie was made for it.

CHOCOLATE CHIP PIE

Preparation time: 15 minutes
Cooking time: 1 hour 10 minutes
Serves: 8

Chef: Aija Eglité
Yacht: Rhapsody

1 cup shortening or butter
1/2 cup brown sugar
1/2 cup granulated sugar
1 tsp. vanilla
2 eggs
2 cups flour, sifted
1 tsp. baking soda
1 tsp. salt
2 cups semi-sweet chocolate morsels
1 cup walnuts, chopped
9-inch deep dish pie shell
Garnish: vanilla ice cream and chocolate shavings

Preheat oven to 350 degrees F.
Cream shortening with sugars and vanilla until light and fluffy. Beat in eggs one at a time. Combine flour, baking soda and salt, blend into sugar mixture. Stir in chocolate morsels and nuts. Spoon into pie shell. Bake for 10 minutes, reduce temperature to 250 degrees F. and bake 60 minutes more. *Serve at room temperature, top with vanilla ice cream and chocolate shavings.*

Vary crusts by adding finely ground walnuts, pecans, filberts or almonds to the crumbs, or add a teaspoon or two of brandy, fruit liqueur or rum.

CHOCOLATE MOUSSE PIE

Preparation time: 30 minutes   *Chef: Debbie Rae*
Cooking time: 20 minutes   *Yacht: Cerulean*
Freezing time: 2 hours
Serves: 8

1 Almond Pie Shell (see page 219)
32 oz. semi-sweet chocolate morsels
1/2 cup prepared Espresso coffee
1/2 cup Grand Marnier
4 egg yolks
1 cup heavy cream, chilled
1/4 cup sugar
8 egg whites
Pinch of salt
1/2 tsp. vanilla extract
Garnish: chocolate leaf molds,
   2 oz. semi-sweet chocolate,
   2 Tblsp. Grand Marnier

Melt chocolate in a large, heavy saucepan over very low heat, stir in coffee and Grand Marnier. Cool to room temperature, add egg yolks one at a time, beating after each addition. In a bowl whip the cream until thick, gradually add sugar, beat until stiff. In another bowl beat egg whites with salt until stiff. Gently fold egg whites into cream. Stir about 1/3 of cream and egg mixture into chocolate, mix thoroughly. Fold remaining egg and cream into chocolate. Pour into an almond pie shell or serving bowl and freeze for 2 hours until set. *Garnish pie with the chocolate leaves below.*

Chocolate Leaves: melt chocolate with Grand Marnier, pour into leaf molds and freeze until firm.

Note: *This is also my* **Chocolate Mousse** *recipe.*

MOCHA CHEESE PIE

Preparation time: 20 minutes   *Chef: Connie Frey*
Chilling time: 1 hour   *Yacht: Jewell*
Serves: 8

1 (8 oz.) pkg. cream cheese
Milk
1 (3.5 oz.) pkg. chocolate instant pudding mix
2-1/2 tsp. instant coffee mix
9-inch graham cracker pie shell (see page 221)
Garnish: whipped cream

Beat cream cheese until smooth and creamy. Beat in 1/4 cup less milk than label on pudding mix directs for basic pudding. Add pudding mix and instant coffee, beating until slightly thickened. Pour into shell and refrigerate. *Serve topped with whipped cream.*

Pie freezes well; serve partially thawed.

DERBY PIE

Preparation time: 15 minutes   *Chef: Vivian Phelps*
Cooking time: 1 hour   *Yacht: Encore*
Serves: 8

2 eggs
1/2 cup flour
1/2 cup sugar
1/2 cup brown sugar
1 cup margarine, softened
1 (12 oz.) pkg. semi-sweet chocolate morsels
1 cup pecans, chopped
9-inch pie shell, uncooked

Preheat oven to 325 degrees F.
Beat eggs until foamy. Beat in flour, sugar and brown sugar. Blend in melted margarine, stir in chocolate morsels and nuts. Pour into pie shell and bake for one hour. *This recipe freezes well.*

KENTUCKY DERBY PIE

Preparation time: 30 minutes　　　　*Chef: Kelly Reed*
Cooking time: 40 minutes　　　　　*Yacht: Capricious*
Serves: 8

2 eggs at room temperature
2 cups sugar
1/2 cup flour
1/2 cup unsalted butter, melted and cooled
1 cup chocolate morsels
1 cup pecans, chopped
1 Tblsp. bourbon (optional)
1 tsp. vanilla
9-inch pie shell, unbaked

Preheat oven to 350 degrees F.
With mixer, beat eggs until light lemon colored. Gradually beat in sugar, reduce speed, add flour and butter, mix well. Stir in chocolate morsels, nuts, bourbon and vanilla. Turn into pie shell and bake.

This pie is good both hot and cold!

This should satisfy everyone's sweet tooth!

MARBLE PETAL PIE

Preparation time: 30 minutes　　　　*Chef: Connie Frey*
Cooking time: 10 minutes　　　　　　*Yacht: Jewell*
Cooling time: 30 minutes
Serves: 6-8

1 pkg. sugar cookies, refrigerated slice 'n bake variety
1 (3.5 oz.) pkg. chocolate instant pudding mix
1 (3.5 oz.) pkg. vanilla instant pudding mix
Milk

Preheat oven to 375 degrees F.
Slice sugar cookies 1/8 inch thick, enough to line the bottom of a 9-inch pie plate, laying slices 1/4 inch apart. Bake 8-10 minutes or until done, cool. In separate bowls prepare both pudding mixes as directed on package labels. When pie shell is cool, spoon the two puddings into the pie shell alternating the two. Swirl with spoon to give a marblized effect.

Refrigerate until serving time.

How to make four flavors with two pies. Build up bottom crust across the middle, making a ridge. Bake half chocolate and half lemon for one pie, half apple and half peach for other, or whatever combinations you want.

LEMON FLUFF

Preparation time: 10 minutes   *Chef: Marion Vanderwood*
Chilling time: 2-3 hours   *Yacht: Ocean Voyager*
Serves: 4-6

1 cup lemon juice, fresh squeezed (about 2 lemons)
1 pkg. lemon gelatin mix
1 (16 oz.) can evaporated milk, frozen
9 inch prepared butter crust
Garnish: lemon slices and extra crumbs of butter crust

Heat lemon juice. Dissolve lemon gelatin into juice, let cool. Whip frozen evaporated milk with gelatin mix until foamy, about 6 minutes. Pour into pie shell, sprinkle some butter crumbs on top. Garnish with lemon slices and chill 2-3 hours. *A nice low calorie, light pie after a heavy meal.*

FROZEN LIME PIE

Preparation time: 30 minutes   *Chef: Wendy Smith*
Freezing time: 3-4 hours   *Yacht: Hiya*
Serves: 6

9-inch graham cracker pie crust (see page 221)
3 eggs, separated
1/2 cup sugar
1 cup whipped cream
2 tsp. grated lemon rind
1/4 cup lime juice
Garnish: slices of lime

Beat the egg whites until frothy, gradually add the sugar and beat until stiff and glossy. Beat yolks until thick and lemon colored, fold into the egg white mixture. Fold lemon rind and lime juice into egg mixture along with the whipped cream. Pour into the pie shell and freeze. *Garnish with lime slices before serving.*

KIWI LIME CHIFFON PIE

Preparation time: 15 minutes   *Chef: Marion Vanderwood*
Chilling time: 2-3 hours   *Yacht: Ocean Voyager*
Serves: 4-6

4 kiwi fruit, peeled and circle sliced
1 graham cracker pie shell (see page 221)
1 (3 oz.) pkg. lime gelatin
Juice of two limes, fresh squeezed
1/3 cup evaporated milk, well chilled
3/4 cup low-fat plain yogurt
Garnish: kiwi fruit slices

Place two sliced kiwis (about 10 slices) on the bottom of pie shell. In saucepan, mix together lime gelatin and lime juice, heat and stir until dissolved. Place gelatin mixture in the freezer until the consistency of egg whites (about 20 minutes). Whip gelatin mixture with cold or frozen evaporated milk for 5 minutes or until foamy, fold in yogurt. Pour into pie shell and lay remaining kiwi slices on top. *Chill 2 to 3 hours.*

This is a great low calorie pie. If sliced into 6 slices, each slice contains only 100 calories. Very light after a heavy dinner.

ISLAND LIME PIE

Preparation time: 10 minutes
Cooking time: 10-15 minutes
Chilling time: 30 minutes
Serves: 6-8

Chef: Candice Carson
Yacht: Freight Train II

1 can sweetened condensed milk
4 eggs, separated
1/2 cup lime juice
6 Tblsp. sugar
1/2 tsp. cream of tartar
9-inch pie shell, baked

Preheat oven to 350 degrees F.
Mix milk and egg yolks, add lime juice. Beat one egg white until stiff, fold into lime juice mixture. Pour into pie shell. Prepare the meringue by beating 3 egg whites and gradually add sugar and cream of tartar. Spread on top of pie and bake just until egg whites are golden. *Refrigerate.*

KEY LIME PIE

Preparation time: 20 minutes
Cooking time: 5-15 minutes
Chilling time: 30 minutes
Serves: 6

Chef: Ninia Cunningham
Yacht: Iona of the Islands

4 eggs, separated
1 (14 oz.) can sweetened condensed milk
3/4 cup fresh lime juice
Zest of lime
9-inch pie shell, baked and cooled
3/4 cup sugar
1 tsp. vanilla

Preheat oven to 425 degrees F.
Beat egg yolks until creamy. Fold in condensed milk, beat lightly. Stir in lime juice and zest, when thickened pour into pie shell. Beat egg whites until very stiff and peaks form. Slowly add sugar. Add vanilla when all the sugar is added. Spread over pie, raising peaks with back of spoon. Brown under broiler until meringue is set and golden, or bake in hot oven (over 425 degrees F.) until set and golden. *Chill before serving.*

Tip: *Insert toothpicks around the pastry shell before wrapping pie with aluminum foil. This prevents meringue from becoming crushed in the refrigerator.*

To make the best meringues, egg whites should be at room temperature to achieve maximum velum. Beat in a copper, stainless or glass bowl. Do not underbeat, or th structure will be unstable and collapse when baked.

SOUR CREAM LIME TARTE

Preparation time: 35 minutes
Cooking time: 10 minutes
Chilling time: 2 hours
Serves: 8

Chef: Joanne Zanusso
Yacht: Serenity

Crust: 1-3/4 cups crushed graham crackers,
or wheatmeal biscuits
1/2 cup sugar
1 Tblsp. fresh lime juice
6 Tblsp. butter, melted
Grated lime peel
Filling: 1 cup sugar
3 Tblsp. cornstarch
1 cup whipping cream
1/3 cup fresh lime juice
1/4 cup butter
2 Tblsp. grated lime peel
1 cup sour cream
Topping: 1 cup whipping cream
1/4 cup sugar
3/4 cup sour cream
Garnish: several thin slices of lime
cut halfway and twisted

Preheat oven to 350 degrees F.
Crust: Mix ingredients together and press into a 9-inch springform or pie pan. Freeze for 10 minutes, bake for 10-12 minutes, or until lightly browned, cool.
Filling: Mix sugar and cornstarch in saucepan over medium heat. Stir in cream, lime juice, butter and peel, boil and whisk until thick, then simmer and stir 5-10 minutes. Cool, fold in sour cream, pour into crust.
Topping: Whip the cream until stiff, add sugar, then fold in sour cream. Spread over filling. Chill for at least 2 hours before serving. *This is refreshing but rich!!*

*One guests snuck ashore at Peter Island to pick limes and then **squeezed** them so I would make it twice.*

STRAWBERRY MARSHMALLOW DELIGHT

Preparation time: 20 minutes *Chef: Marion Vanderwood*
Chilling time: 2-3 hours *Yacht: Ocean Voyager*
Serves: 6

1 graham cracker pie crust (see page 221)
1/4 cup brown sugar
1/4 cup butter, melted
1/2 cup milk
24 large marshmallows
1 cup boiling water
1 (3 oz.) pkg. strawberry gelatin
16 oz. frozen strawberries
1-1/4 cups whipped cream
Garnish: strawberries

Crush graham cracker crust. Mix crumbs, brown sugar and butter, press into bottom of a square pan. Slowly heat milk and marshmallows, let cool. Mix boiling water, gelatin and frozen strawberries, allow to cool.When almost set spread onto crust. When marshmallow mix is cool, beat together with whipped cream and pour on top of strawberry mixture. *Chill 2-3 hours.*

To serve: cut into squares and garnish each piece with a few strawberries.

Put a layer of marshmallows in the bottom of a pumpkin pie, then add filling. When it's cooked, you will have a nice topping, as the marshmallow will rise to the top.

TANGY MARSHMALLOW PIE

Preparation time: 20 minutes *Chef: Connie Frey*
Chilling time: 4 hours *Yacht: Jewell*
Serves: 8

36 large marshmallows
3/4 cup orange juice
1 (2 oz.) env. dessert-topping mix
9-inch pie shell, baked and cooled

In a large saucepan combine marshmallows and orange juice, cook over low heat, stirring, just until marshmallows melt into juice. Transfer to a bowl, refrigerate until mixture mounds slightly when dropped from a spoon. Prepare the dessert-topping mix as directed on package. Fold 1-1/2 cups of it into the marshmallow mixture. Pour into pie shell and refrigerate for at least 4 hours.

Serve topped with remaining dessert-topping.

MACADAMIA CHIFFON PIE

Preparation time: 20 minutes
Chilling time: 6 hours
Serves: 8

Chef: Nancy May
Yacht: Tri My Way

3/4 cup packed brown sugar
1 env. gelatin, unflavored
1/4 tsp. salt
1 cup milk
2 eggs (separated)
1 tsp. vanilla
1/2 cup macadamia nuts,
   chopped and toasted
9-inch pie shell, baked
Garnish: 1/2 cup whipped cream
   and macadamia nuts

In saucepan combine 1/2 cup brown sugar, gelatin and salt. Stir in milk and slightly beaten egg yolks. Cook over medium heat until mixture thickens, stirring constantly. Remove from heat, stir in vanilla. Chill 15 minutes, stir occasionally. Beat egg whites until stiff, gradually add remaining brown sugar. Fold egg whites into gelatin mixture, add nuts; (reserve some for garnish) pile into pie shell. Chill for 6 hours.

Serve with whipped cream on top and sprinkle with remaining macadamia nuts.

To avoid lumpy gelatin mixtures, sprinkle unflavored gelatine over cold water; let stand 1 minute. Cook and stir over low heat until dissolved

PEANUT BUTTER CREAM PIE

Preparation time: 5 minutes
Chilling time: 1 hour
Serves: 8

Chef: John Freeman
Yacht: Solid Gold, Too

1 (8 oz.) pkg. cream cheese
1 tsp. lemon juice
1/4 tsp. vanilla extract
2 Tblsp. brown sugar
1-1/4 cup chunky peanut butter
1 cup whipping cream
1 env. unflavored gelatin, dissolved
9-inch graham cracker pie crust (see page 221)
Garnish: 1/4 cup Cool Whip and
1 tsp. grated sweet chocolate

In a food processor cream together the cream cheese, lemon juice, vanilla and brown sugar until light in texture. Add peanut butter, blend for 30 seconds. Add cream, blend for 30 seconds. Add dissolved, warm gelatin blend for 20 seconds. Pour mixture into pie crust and refrigerate for 1 hour. *Garnish with Cool Whip and sprinkle with grated chocolate.*

An interesting variation would be to serve the pie on a lake of chocolate syrup or fruit puree.

If chilled dough is too stiff to roll, allow it to stand at room temperature until it becomes more workable.

MICROWAVE PECAN PIE

Preparation time: 2 minutes
Cooking time: 9 minutes (microwave)
Serves: 6-8

Chef: Jan Robinson
Yacht: Vanity

1/4 cup unsalted butter
1-1/2 cup pecan halves
1 cup sugar
1/2 cup light or dark corn syrup
3 eggs, lightly beaten
1 tsp. vanilla
1 baked 9-inch pie shell, in microwave safe pie dish
Garnish: vanilla ice cream

Melt butter in 2-quart microwave safe measuring bowl on High. Add nuts, sugar, corn syrup, eggs, and vanilla and blend well. Pour into pie shell. Cook on High until center is set, about 8 to 9 minutes.

Serve either at room temperature or chilled, with ice cream.

If ice cream is too hard to scoop easily, loosen top of container and microwave on medium (50% power) for 45-60 seconds, depending on hardness. Of course, we don't usually have that problem on a boat!

PECAN PIE

Preparation time: 10 minutes
Cooking time: 50 minutes
Serves: 6

Chef: Carol Cutler
Yacht: Got Lucky, Too

3 eggs, beaten
1 cup dark Karo Syrup
1 cup sugar
Pinch salt
1 tsp. vanilla
2 tsp. butter, melted
1 cup pecan halves
9-inch pie shell, unbaked

Preheat oven to 400 degrees F.
Mix together first 6 ingredients. Stir well, fold in pecans.
Pour into pie shell and bake 15 minutes. Reduce heat to
350 degrees F. and bake for 30-35 minutes longer.

This is always a favorite.

BARBADOS RUM WALNUT PIE

Preparation time: 30 minutes
Cooking time: 45 minutes
Chilling time: 30 minutes
Serves: 8-10

Chef: Allison Moir
Yacht: Pride of Lyn

Crust: 1/2 cup butter, softened
   3 Tblsp. dark brown sugar
   1/2 cup walnuts, finely chopped
   1 egg, beaten
   1/2 tsp. almond extract
   1-1/3 cups flour
Filling: 4 eggs
   3/4 cup dark brown sugar
   1 cup light corn syrup
   1/3 cup dark rum
   1/4 cup butter, melted
   2 cups walnuts, chopped and toasted
Topping: 1 cup whipped cream
   1 Tblsp. powdered sugar
   1 Tblsp. rum

Preheat oven to 350 degrees F.

Crust: Grease a 10 inch springform pan. Cream butter and sugar in a bowl, add nuts, egg and extract. Mix in flour and blend. Press dough into pan, spreading evenly up the sides about 2 inches. Chill 30 minutes.

Filling: Mix eggs and sugar until creamy. Add syrup and rum, then butter, blend well. Place nuts in pie shell; pour filling over and bake for 45 minutes, or until knife inserted comes out clean and top is golden. Cool, then refrigerate.

Topping: Just before serving, whip cream with powdered sugar and rum. Remove pan sides and spoon on the whipped cream.

Note: *This pie is less rich than the usual pecan pie but is sure to satisfy everyone's sweet-tooth! Works well with a mixture of nuts also.*

DACQUOISE

Preparation time: 30 minutes
Cooking time: 1-2 hours
Serves: 6

Chef: Amanda Baker
Yacht: Gypsy Wind

3 oz. whole almonds, shelled
4 egg whites
1 cup sugar
Pinch of cream of tartar
1 cup raspberries (fresh or frozen)
1 cup heavy cream, with sugar to taste
Garnish: raspberries and powdered sugar

Preheat oven to 275 degrees F.
Blanch almonds, dry well and pass through blender or processor. Whip egg whites until very stiff, fold in sugar, cream of tartar and ground nuts. Cover two baking sheets with waxed paper. Make two rounds of meringue. Bake for 1 to 2 hours, or until meringue peels away from paper. Whip cream until stiff, (save some for piping on top) then fold cream into fruit. Sandwich cream mixture between the two cooled meringues. *Decorate top with remaining cream, raspberries and powdered sugar.*

A light dessert that compliments most meals and it can be made with any fruit available.

Hint: *In case of disaster, break meringue into small pieces and mix with the fruit and cream. Serve in individual dishes and decorate the top...just as delicious!!*

Tap meringues at end of baking time for a hollow sound. If too soft or sticky, bake at same temperature a little longer. Turn off oven, let pie cool 1 hour in closed oven.

EASY BAKED ALASKA

Preparation time: 75 minutes　　　*Chef: Jan Robinson*
Cooking time: 13-15 minutes　　　　*Yacht: Vanity*
Freeze: overnight
Serves: 6-10

Crust:
   1-1/4 cups vanilla wafer crumbs
   1/4 cup finely chopped walnuts
   1/3 cup melted butter
Filling:
   1 pint coffee ice cream, softened
   1 pint chocolate ice cream, softened
Topping:
   5 egg whites
   1/3 tsp. cream of tartar
   6 Tblsp. superfine sugar

Preheat oven to 350 degrees F.
Crust: Prepare the crust by combining crumbs, walnuts and butter. Press into a 9 inch springform pan. Bake for 8-10 minutes. Cool thoroughly.

Filling: Spread coffee and chocolate ice cream into two separate layers, cover and freeze until firm.

Topping: Beat egg whites and cream of tartar until stiff peaks form, gradually add sugar until stiff and glossy. Pile meringue on pie and freeze overnight.

To serve: ten minutes before serving preheat oven to 450 degrees F. Place pie on cookie sheet and bake for 5 minutes or until meringue tips are brown, serve immediately.

Tip: *Make the crust a day ahead. Use ice cream flavors of your choice.*

MILE HIGH LEMON MERINGUE PIE

Preparation time: 30 minutes   *Chef: Vanessa Owen*
Cooking time: 35 minutes   *Yacht: Endless Summer II*
Chillng time: 45 minutes
Serves: 8

Crust: 2 cups flour
1/2 tsp. salt
3/4 cup unsalted butter
3 Tblsp. margarine
1/4 cup ice water
Filling: 1/4 cup corn flour
2-1/2 cups water
6 Tblsp. sugar
Zest and juice of 2 lemons
2 egg yolks
Meringue: 12 egg whites
1/2 tsp. cream of tartar
1/2 tsp. vanilla
Pinch salt
6 Tblsp. sugar

Preheat oven to 350 degrees F.
Crust: Add salt to flour, rub in butter and margarine. Drip water in while turning with a fork. Mold into a ball, wrap and chill. Press into 9-inch pie pan and bake 15 minutes, remove and cool.
Filling: Blend corn flour and 1/2 cup of water in saucepan, add sugar, lemon juice and zest, boil 5 minutes. Add remaining water, stir well, cool then beat in egg yolks. Pour into cooled crust and chill.
Meringue: Beat egg whites until fluffy, add cream of tartar, vanilla, salt. Continue beating, adding sugar gradually. When stiff, spoon into a 'mountain' over filling use back of spoon to form peaks. Bake 15 minutes until lightly browned. Cool but don't refrigerate.

SOURSOP MERINGUE PIE

Preparation time: 15 minutes
Cooking time: 10-15 minutes
Serves: 8

Chef: Judy Knape
Yacht: Endless Summer 48

Filling:
- 4 egg yolks
- 1/4 cup soursop nectar or 1/2 cup fresh squeezed soursop juice and pulp (pureed)
- 2 Tblsp. lime juice
- Zest of 1 lime
- 1 (14 oz.) can sweetened condensed milk
- 9-inch pie shell, baked

Meringue:
- 1 tsp. vanilla
- 4 egg whites
- 1/4 cup sugar
- 1/4 tsp. cream of tartar (optional)

Garnish: lime zest or peel slivers

Preheat oven to 350 degrees F.

Filling: Beat egg yolks until lemon colored, add soursop, lime juice, zest and milk. Beat with electric mixer for 3 minutes. Pour into cooled pie shell.

Meringue: Beat egg whites until almost stiff. Add sugar and vanilla gradually, while beating a brief time more (add and beat in cream of tartar if needed to stiffen egg white mixture). Pour onto filling and make peaks with back of spoon. Bake 10-15 minutes.

Meringues that have lost their crispness can be dried in a preheated 225 degree F. oven for 15-25 minutes.

PARADISE PAVLOVA

Preparation time: 20 minute
Cooking time: 1 hour
Cooling time: 1 hour
Serves: 6

Chef: Jan Robinson
Yacht: Vanity

Meringue:
   4 egg whites
   1/4 tsp. salt
   1 cup sugar
   1 Tblsp. cornstarch
   2 tsp. vinegar
   1/2 tsp. vanilla
Topping:
   1-1/2 cups heavy whipping cream
   1/4 cup sugar
   Fresh fruits (kiwifruit, strawberries, raspberries, etc.)

Preheat oven to 300 degrees F.
Meringue: Prepare a baking tray by lining with foil and greasing with melted butter, or spray with non-stick. Beat the egg whites and salt until soft peaks form when the beater is lifted from the mixture. Add the sugar, a little at a time beating well after each addition. Continue to beat until the mixture is stiff. Add cornstarch, vinegar, and vanilla. Beat thoroughly until very stiff. Pile mixture into a circle about 9 inches in diameter, on the prepared baking tray. Bake for 1 hour. Turn oven off and leave pavlova in the oven with the door closed until pavlova is cool or cold. Remove carefully from the foil and place on a serving plate, preferably a cake stand.
Topping: Just before serving, whip cream with sugar. Spread it over the pavlova. Prepare fruit and arrange on top of cream.

This dessert is always a big hit!! Light and lovely!

BAKED BRIE

Preparation time: 5 minutes   *Chef: Kate Young*
Cooking time: 20 minutes   *Yacht: Alize*
Serves: 6

1 Brie cheese
Phyllo dough
Butter

Preheat oven to 375 degrees F.
Wrap Brie in several layers of Phyllo dough and brush with melted butter. Use your imagination to decorate the top. Try using the dough to make a rose, leaves, grape vine, etc. Bake until golden brown. *Serve with assorted cookies or crackers, white seedless grapes or apple slices. This recipe is fast, beautiful and delicious!*

DANISH PUFF

Preparation time: 15 minutes   *Chef: Ronnie Hochman*
Cooking time: 60 minutes   *Yacht: Illusion II*
Serves: 8

Pastry:
   1 cup flour (sifted)
   1/2 cup margarine
   2 Tblsp. water
Filling:
   1/2 cup margarine
   1 cup water
   1 tsp almond flavoring
   1 cup flour (sifted)
   3 eggs
Garnish: powdered sugar icing and
   chopped nuts (optional)

Preheat oven to 350 degrees F.
Pastry: Cut margarine into flour, sprinkle with water, mix with a fork. Form into a ball and divide in half. Pat dough into 2 long strips, 12x3-inches, and place 3-inches apart on an ungreased baking sheet.

Filling: Bring margarine and water to a rolling boil. Stir in flour immediately to keep from lumping. When mixture is smooth and thick, stir in one egg at a time, beating until smooth. Divide mixture in half, spreading each half evenly over each pastry piece. Bake about 60 minutes until topping is crisp and nicely browned.

You may want to frost with a powdered sugar icing and sprinkle generously with chopped nuts.

PERNOD PASTRIES

Preparation time: 10 minutes   *Chef: Shirley Benjamin*
Cooking time: 20 minutes   *Yacht: Verano Sin Final*
Serves: 8

1 sheet puff pastry
1 (8 oz.) pkg. cream cheese,
  room temperature
Powdered sugar
Lemon juice
Fresh fruit (bananas, peaches or plums),
  or your choice
2 Tblsp. Pernod
1/2 jar apricot preserves
1 Tblsp. butter

Preheat oven to 375 degrees F.
Divide pastry into 8 portions, bake until golden, remove from oven, cool and split each portion in half. Process cream cheese with powdered sugar and lemon juice to taste and spread on pastry squares. Top with a sliced fresh fruit. Heat Pernod, 1/2 jar of apricot preserves and butter;zs drizzle over fruit and top with other half of pastry. *Serve immediately.*

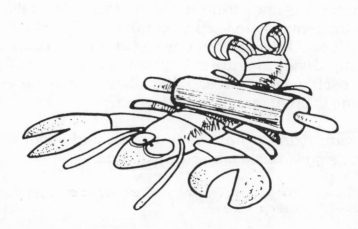

ALMOND PASTRY SHELL

Preparation time: 15 minutes　　　　　*Chef: Debbie Rae*
Cooking time: 12 minutes　　　　　　　*Yacht: Cerulean*
Serves: 8

1/3 cup butter
2-1/2 Tblsp. sugar
1/3 tsp. salt
1 egg yolk
1 cup all-purpose flour
1/3 cup almonds, finely chopped

Preheat oven to 400 degrees F.
Grease a 10-inch pie plate. Cream butter with sugar and salt until fluffy. Add yolk and beat thoroughly, mix in flour and almonds. Press into prepared plate, bake 12 minutes and cool.

This goes great with left over chocolate mousse as a filling (see recipe on page 195 for **Chocolate Mousse Pie**).

*For a tender, flaky crust, **do not** over-flour your rolling surface.*

THE AMAZING FUNGIBLE PIES

Preparation time: 5 minutes   *Chef: Jan Robinson*
Chilling time: 1 hour   *Yacht: Vanity*
Serves: 8

With this basic filling and an unlimited supply of liqueurs, you can create an almost infinite number of pies - each different, all delicious. Choose a **Graham Cracker** *or* **Cookie Crust,** *(page 221 or 222) and proceed as follows:*

Filling:
    1 cup sugar
    1 env. unflavored gelatin
    4 eggs, separated
    1/2 cup water
    Flavorings (suggestions follow)

In a small saucepan, stir together 1/2 cup sugar and gelatin. Blend egg yolks with water and flavorings of your choice. Stir into sugar mixture. Cook over medium heat, stirring constantly, until mixture comes to a boil. Remove from heat, cool and refrigerate; stir occasionally until mixture is cool and thickened. Beat egg white until foamy. Add remaining 1/2 cup sugar, 1 Tblsp. at a time, beating until egg whites form stiff, glossy peaks. Fold gelatin mixture into meringue. Spoon into prebaked 9-inch pie shell.

Black Russian Pie:
1/2 cup vodka
3 Tblsp. coffee liqueur (e.g. Kahlua)

Butterscotch Collins Pie:
    5 Tblsp. Scotch
    2 Tblsp. Scotch liqueur (e.g. Drambuie)
    1 Tblsp. lemon juice
    Garnish: orange slices and cherries

THE AMAZING FUNGIBLE PIES (cont'd)

The Great Brandy Alexander Pie:
 1/3 cup brandy
 3 Tblsp. Creme de Cacao

Gimlet Pie:
 1/3 cup gin or vodka
 2 Tblsp. lime juice
 Grated peel of 1 lime
 Juice of 1/2 lime

Lemon Lime Daiquiri Pie:
 1/3 cup golden rum
 2 Tblsp. fresh lime juice
 1 Tblsp. fresh lemon juice

Comin' Thru The Rye Pie:
 1/4 cup rye or bourbon whiskey
 1/4 cup fresh orange juice
 2 Tblsp. grated orange peel

GRAHAM CRACKER CRUST

Preparation time: 5 minutes
Cooking time: 8 to 10 minutes
Chilling time: 45 minutes
Makes: 9-inch pie shell

Chef: Jan Robinson
Yacht: Vanity

20 graham cracker squares
1/4 cup sugar
1/4 tsp. cinnamon
6 Tblsp. butter or margarine, melted

Crush the graham crackers into very fine crumbs to measure 1-1/2 cups. Place crumbs in medium bowl; stir in sugar and cinnamon, add butter; mix well. Turn the mixture into a 9-inch pie plate, spread evenly, pat onto the sides and bottom to form a firm even crust. Chill. Or, bake in a 375 degrees F. oven. *Cool before filling.*

COOKIE CRUST

Preparation time: 5 minutes   *Chef: Jan Robinson*
Cooking time: 10 minutes   *Yacht: Vanity*
Makes: 9-inch pie shell

1-1/2 cups cookies, crushed
  (vanilla or chocolate wafers, or gingersnaps)
1/4 cup (1/2 stick) butter, melted

Preheat oven to 350 degrees F. Select crushed cookie. Mix all ingredients together and press into a 9-inch pie plate. Bake 10 minutes, allow to cool.

WHOLE WHEAT PIE SHELL

Preparation time: 7 minutes   *Chef: Nancy May*
Chilling time: 30 minutes   *Yacht: Tri My Way*
Cooking time: 10-15 minutes
Makes: Two 10-inch shells

1 cup unbleached flour
1 cup whole wheat pastry flour
2/3 cup chilled butter
Dash salt
4-6 Tblsp. ice water

Preheat oven to 400 degrees F.
Combine flours, cut in butter and salt, just enough to break butter into small pieces. Add ice water, mixing well but quickly. Divide dough in half and chill. To use, roll out and place in two 10-inch pie pans. Bake 10-15 minutes.

Hint: *The trick to a good pie crust is not to overhandle the dough.*

PASTRY FOR A SINGLE-CRUST PIE

Preparation time: 15 minutes   *Chef: Jan Robinson*
Cooking time: 10-12 minutes   *Yacht: Vanity*
Makes: one 9-inch pie shell

1-1/4 cups all-purpose flour
1/2 tsp. salt
1/3 cup shortening or lard
3 to 4 Tblsp. cold water

Stir together flour and salt. cut in shortening until pieces are the size of small peas. Sprinkle 1 Tblsp. water over part of the mixture; gently toss with a fork. Push to side of bowl; repeat procedure till all is moistened. Form dough into a ball.

On a lightly floured surface, flatten dough with hands. Roll from center to edge, forming a circle about 12-inches in diameter. Wrap pastry around rolling pin. Unroll onto a 9-inch pie plate. Ease pastry into pie plate, being careful to avoid stretching pastry. Trim edge 1/2 to 1 inch beyond edge of pie plate; fold excess under, then flute edge.

Note: *For a baked pie shell, prick bottom and sides. Bake in 450 degrees F. oven for 10 to 12 minutes.*

Paint top crust of fruit pies with milk or cream and dust with sugar for a glaze. To prevent edge of crust from over browning, cover edge of pastry with strip of foil. Remove during last 15 minutes of baking.

Notes

PUDDINGS AND SAUCES

Notes

BAKED CUSTARD

Preparation time: 15 minutes
Cooking time: 45-60 minutes
Cooling time: 30 minutes
Serves: 6

Chef: Wendy Smith
Yacht: Hiya

1 cup sugar
3 eggs
3 egg yolks
1-1/4 cups heavy cream
1-1/4 cups milk
1 vanilla bean (split)
1/4 cup dried apricots, chopped
1/4 cup raisins
Nutmeg

Preheat oven to 325 degrees F.
Whisk together sugar, eggs and egg yolks until pale yellow and creamy. In a small saucepan, combine the cream, milk and vanilla bean, bring to a boil. Butter six ramekins or a 1-1/2 quart shallow baking dish. Remove vanilla bean. Pour the two mixtures together and then pour into the bowls or baking dish. Sprinkle with apricots, raisins and nutmeg. Put dishes into a larger pan with 1 inch of hot water. Bake until set. *Cool before serving.*

OH NO, It's Beating Time!

CINNAMON RAISIN CUSTARD

Preparation time: 15 minutes
Cooking time: 25 minutes
Cooling time: 15 minutes
Serves: 8-10

Chef: Aija Eglité
Yacht: Rhapsody

16 slices cinnamon-raisin bread
1 stick (4 oz.) butter, melted
4 whole eggs
1 egg yolk
1/2 cup sugar
2 cups milk
1 cup heavy cream
1 Tblsp. vanilla extract
Garnish: 2 cups assorted berries, powdered sugar

Preheat oven to 350 degrees F.
Butter a 9x12 inch pan. Brush both sides of bread slices with melted butter, arrange in two layers in pan. Beat together eggs and yolk. Whisk in sugar, milk, cream and vanilla. Pour over bread slices. Place the pan in a larger pan of warm water and bake 25 minutes until set and lightly browned. Allow to stand 10-15 minutes before slicing. *To serve, sprinkle with powdered sugar and top with fresh berries.*

Hint: *Drained frozen berries may be substituted. Great for dessert or as a sweet start to the day!*

BRANDIED PUMPKIN FLAN

Preparation time: 30 minutes   *Chef: Joanne Zanusso*
Cooking time: 50 minutes   *Yacht: Serenity*
Serves: 8

3/4 cup sugar, caramelized
1 cup canned pumpkin
1 cup milk
1 cup light cream
6 eggs
1/2 cup sugar
2 tsp. vanilla
1/3 cup brandy
3 Tblsp. brandy for flambé (optional)
Garnish: sliced almonds and 1 cup whipped cream

Preheat oven to 350 degrees F.

Caramelize: Place sugar in a large saucepan over medium heat until sugar melts and forms a light brown syrup. (Watch it closely, as sugar browns fast and burns easily). Immediately pour the syrup into a warm 8 or 9-inch round shallow baking dish. Rotate to cover bottom and side.

In a medium saucepan, combine pumpkin, milk and cream. Stir over medium heat until bubbly. In a bowl, beat eggs lightly, add sugar and vanilla. Add 3 tablespoons of hot milk mixture to egg mixture, then slowly add back to hot milk mixture while stirring. Add brandy. Pour into baking dish. Set dish in shallow pan and add a hot water bath until 1/2 inch level around dish. Bake until firm, about 50 minutes (a knife inserted in center should come out clean.) Cool and refrigerate if desired.

To serve: run knife around edge and release onto a serving dish. Syrup will run around edge. Decorate with almonds. Pour 3 tablespoons of brandy over flan and ignite to flambe. Top with whipped cream. If you flambé dessert it is spectacular!

AMARETTO RICE PUDDING

Preparation time: 10 minutes   *Chef: Jan Robinson*
Cooking time: 1 hour 30 minutes   *Yacht:Vanity*
Serves: 6

3 eggs, beaten
2/3 cup water
1/4 tsp. salt
2 cups milk, scalded
1-1/2 cups cooked rice
1/4 tsp. cinnamon
1/3 cup Amaretto
1 tsp. vanilla
1/4 tsp. ground nutmeg

Preheat oven to 325 degrees F.
Combine eggs, water and salt in a medium bowl. Slowly add milk, stirring constantly. Stir in rice, cinnamon, Amaretto and vanilla. Spoon mixture into a buttered 1-1/2 quart baking dish. Place dish in a large, shallow pan. Add 1 inch of hot water to the pan and bake 1 hour. Stir mixture, then sprinkle evenly with nutmeg. Bake 30 additional minutes. *Remove baking dish from pan, cool and serve.*

FLUFFY RICE PUDDING

Preparation time: 10 minutes
Cooking time: 30 minutes
Chilling time: 45 minutes
Serves: 6

Chef: Jan Robinson
Yacht: Vanity

3/4 cup long grain rice
1/4 cup sugar
4 cups milk
1/4 cup dry sherry or milk
1-1/2 tsp. vanilla
1/4 tsp. almond extract
1/2 cup whipping cream

In a heavy 2-quart saucepan combine rice and sugar. Stir in 4 cups milk; bring mixture to boiling. Reduce heat, cover and cook 25 to 30 minutes, or till rice is tender, stirring occasionally. Stir in the 1/4 cup sherry or milk, the vanilla and almond extract. Cool to room temperature. Whip cream to soft peaks and fold into rice mixture. Cover and chill thoroughly.

Note: *As a special treat; spoon rice pudding into sherbet dishes and drizzle* **Rasberry Sauce** *(see below) over each serving.*

Raspberry Sauce:
1 (10 oz.) pkg. frozen red raspberries, thawed
1 Tblsp. cornstarch
1/2 cup currant jelly

In a saucepan crush raspberries. Stir in cornstarch and add currant jelly. Cook and stir until mixture is thickened and bubbly; cook 1 minute more. Sieve sauce; discard seeds. Cover surface of sauce with waxed paper or plastic wrap. *Cool sauce to room temperature.*

APPLE GINGER PUDDING

Preparation time: 15 minutes
Cooking time: 30-40 minutes
Serves: 6

Chef: Peggy Curren
Yacht: Traveline

4 large apples
2 Tblsp. butter
Grated rind and juice of 1/2 lemon
1/2 cup brown sugar
1 (7 oz.) box ginger snaps, broken to bite-size pieces
1 cup whipping cream

Preheat oven to 350 degrees F.
Peel, core and slice apples. In large frying pan, heat butter on medium high. Saute apples until slightly softened (3-4 minutes). Add grated lemon rind, juice and 1/3 cup of the brown sugar, cook until sugar dissolves. In a buttered 6 cup souffle or gratin dish, arrange a layer of cookies, cover with apple mixture and pour on layer of cream. Continue until dish is full, finishing with cream. Sprinkle with remaining brown sugar. Cover with foil and bake for 30-40 minutes or until apples are soft. *Serve hot.*

Hint: *You may substitute pears for the apples and chocolate wafers for the ginger snaps for* **Pear Chocolate Pudding.**

ISLAND BANANA PUDDING

Preparation time: 20 minutes　　　*Chef: Jan Robinson*
Cooking time: 15 minutes　　　　　*Yacht: Vanity*
Serves: 12

6 ripe bananas, sliced
1 box vanilla wafers
2 pkgs. vanilla pudding
4 cups milk
1 large can crushed pineapple
Garnish: whipped cream

Drain pineapple and save juice. Layer vanilla wafers, then bananas in the bottom of a flat glass dish. Cook both of the puddings with 4 cups milk, as per package directions. Pour one half on the layers. Add another layer of wafers and bananas; put 1/2 of the pineapple on top of the bananas. Pour rest of pudding on top. One more layer of wafers, bananas and top with the rest of pineapple plus the juice. Let it cool, but do not chill. *Cut into squares and serve with whipped cream.*

Note:*This is a great pudding to take on a picnic, minus the whipped cream.*

_ *I wouldn't go for this recipe, you'll get creamed man!*

CHOCOLATE PUDDING

Preparation time: 15 minutes   *Chef: Jan Robinson*
Cooking time: 10-15 minutes   *Yacht: Vanity*
Chilling time: 30 minutes
Serves: 4

1 cup sugar
2 Tblsp. cornstarch
1/4 tsp. salt
2 cups milk
2 squares (2 oz.) unsweetened chocolate
1 egg, well beaten
2 Tblsp. butter or margarine
1 tsp. vanilla

In a saucepan combine the sugar, cornstarch and salt. Stir in milk. Chop the chocolate and stir it in. Cook and stir over medium heat till mixture is thickened and bubbly, then stir and cook 2 minutes more. Remove from heat. Gradually blend 1 cup of hot mixture into egg, then slowly add this into mixture in saucepan. Stir and cook 2 minutes. Remove from heat; stir in butter and vanilla. Cool. Pour mixture into sherbet or dessert dishes and chill.

Note: *To make* **Vanilla Pudding** *follow recipe as above, except reduce sugar to 3/4 cup and omit chocolate. Or, for* **Chocolate Mocha Pudding,** *dissolve 1 Tblsp. instant coffee in 1/2 Tblsp. hot water, add with milk in recipe.*

CHOCOLATE MINT TAPIOCA

Preparation time: 5 minutes
Cooking time: 5-10 minutes
Chilling time: 30 minutes
Serves: 6-8

Chef: Judy Knape
Yacht: Endless Summer 48

2 pkgs. vanilla tapioca pudding
4 cups milk
2 Tblsp. cocoa
2 Tblsp. chocolate-mint instant coffee mix
** or try flavors of your choice**
1 Tblsp. Kahlua
Garnish: chocolate mint patties and whipped cream

Combine all ingredients in a saucepan, whisk together over medium-high heat and bring to a boil. Cook 2-3 minutes, stirring constantly. Pour into individual serving cups or parfait glasses, let cool and refrigerate. *Serve with a dollop of whipped cream and mint patties.*

To keep a 'skin' from forming on top of a pudding mixture while cooling, carefully place a piece of clear plastic wrap or waxed paper directly on the surface of hot pudding. After pudding has cooled, remove paper and spoon pudding into dessert dishes to serve.

CHOCOLATE BREAD PUDDING

Preparation time: 10 minutes
Cooking time: 1 hour 10 minutes
Serves: 6-8

Chef: Jan Robinson
Yacht: Vanity

4 eggs, beaten
2-2/3 cups milk
1/2 cup sugar
1-1/2 tsp. vanilla
1 tsp. ground cinnamon
1/2 tsp. salt
4 cups dry bread cubes
3/4 cup tiny semi-sweet chocolate pieces
1/3 cup walnuts, chopped

Preheat oven to 350 degrees F.
In a mixing bowl, combine eggs, milk, sugar, vanilla, cinnamon and salt. Stir in bread cubes, chocolate and nuts. Pour into an ungreased 10x6x2-inch baking dish. Place dish in larger baking pan with 1-inch of hot water. Bake 65 to 70 minutes, or until a knife inserted comes out clean. *Serve warm.*

Note: *Also good served with* **Custard Sauce** *(see page 251).*

FRENCH BREAD PUDDING
WITH WHISKEY SAUCE

Preparation time: 30 minutes   *Chef: Nancy May*
Cooking time: 45 minutes   *Yacht: Tri My Way*
Serves: 6-8

1 stick (4 oz.) butter, softened
1 cup sugar
5 eggs, beaten
2 cups heavy cream
1 Tblsp. vanilla
Dash cinnamon
1/2 cup raisins, more if desired
10 slices French bread, in 1 inch slices
Whiskey Sauce, recipe follows

Preheat oven to 350 degrees F.
Beat butter and sugar until creamy. Add eggs, cream, vanilla and cinnamon, beat until smooth. Stir in raisins. Pour into a greased 9-inch square or 9x12-inch glass baking dish. Place bread in dish for 5 minutes to soak up liquid, turn over and let stand 10 minutes. Put dish into a larger pan of water. Cover pudding with foil and bake 35 minutes. Uncover and bake 10 minutes more, until lightly browned (pudding is still soft). *To serve, spoon pudding onto plates and drizzle with Whiskey Sauce.*

Whiskey Sauce:
**   1 cup heavy cream**
**   1 cup sugar**
**   Pinch cinnamon**
**   1 Tblsp. butter**
**   1/2 tsp. cornstarch, dissolved in 1/4 cup water**
**   1-2 Tblsp. bourbon**

In medium saucepan combine cream, sugar, butter and cinnamon. Bring to a boil, stirring frequently to dissolve sugar. Stir in cornstarch mixture, cook until sauce thickens. Remove from heat and stir in bourbon. *Serve warm.*

STEAMED CHOCOLATE PUDDING
WITH SAUCE

Preparation time: 45 minutes
Cooking time: 2 hours
Serves: 6-8

Chef: Jan Robinson
Yacht: Vanity

2 cups sifted flour
2 tsp. baking powder
1/2 tsp. soda
1/4 tsp. salt
1/3 cup butter
1/2 cup sugar
1 egg, beaten well
3 squares unsweetened chocolate, melted
1 cup milk

1/4 cup brown sugar, sifted
1 egg yolk
dash of salt
1 egg white
1/4 cup cream, whipped
1/2 tsp. vanilla

Pudding: Mix ingredients in order, mixing well between each addition. Turn into greased mold. (If mold does not have a cover, cover tightly with tin foil. A tin can may be used also covered with foil.) Steam for 2 hours.

Sauce: Add 1/2 cup of sugar to egg yolk and beat until light. Add salt to egg white and beat until foamy. Combine remaining sugar with whipped cream. Mix these 3 mixtures together. Serve over hot pudding.

CREAMY PEANUT BUTTER PUDDING

Preparation time: 5 minutes
Cooking time: 10 minutes
Serves: 4

Chef: Jan Robinson
Yacht: Vanity

2 Tblsp. cornstarch
1/2 cup milk
1-1/2 cups milk
1/4 cup peanut butter
1/4 cup honey
1/8 tsp. salt
1 egg, beaten
1 tsp. vanilla

In a small bowl, blend cornstarch with 1/2 cup milk. In a saucepan, over moderate heat, heat remaining 1-1/2 cups milk. When milk is almost boiling, add peanut butter, honey and salt. Mix thoroughly, then stir in cornstarch mixture and continue cooking about 5 minutes, until thick and creamy. Pour about 1/2 cup of the hot mixture into the beaten egg, then return this mixture to the saucepan and cook 1 minute longer. Remove pan from heat, add vanilla and beat about 1 minute. Cool. Pour into individual dessert dishes, cover and refrigerate several hours before serving.

RICH BREAD PUDDING AND RUM SAUCE

Preparation time: 20 minutes   *Chef:Jan Robinson*
Cooking time: 12 minutes (microwave)   *Yacht: Vanity*
Serves: 6

**1 oz. butter
3 slices very dry bread, with crusts
1/3 cup milk
1/2 cup cream
1/2 cup brown or white sugar
1 egg, plus 1 egg white
1 tsp. vanilla
1/4 cup of raisins or sultanas
1/4 cup walnuts or almonds
1/4 tsp. each of cinnamon, allspice, grated nutmeg**

In a bowl, melt butter in microwave at full power, 1-2 minutes. Add bread, broken into small pieces. Mix milk and cream; add sugar, egg, egg white, and vanilla. Pour over the bread, then combine gently with a fork. Add raisins, nuts and spices, mix again. (The mixture should be firm enough to hold a rounded shape. Add extra milk or bread if necessary). Spoon into 6 ramekins. Sprinkle surface with nutmeg. Arrange dishes in a circle around the edge of the microwave turntable. Microwave, uncovered, at medium power (50%), 8-10 minutes or until firm. *The pudding is better if bread is stale. If fresh use a second egg.*

Rum Sauce:
    **2 oz. butter
    3/4 cup powdered sugar
    1 egg yolk
    3 Tblsp. rum**

Melt butter on full power in microwave for 1 minute. Beat in sugar and egg yolk. Microwave 30 seconds, or until it bubbles. Cool then stir in rum. *Serve with Bread Pudding.*

Note:*Sauce lovers double the quantity! Make it with dark rum, whiskey, brandy, or bourbon.*

HOT FUDGE PUDDING

Preparation time: 10 minutes
Cooking time: 45 minutes
Serves: 6

Chef: Ronnie Hochman
Yacht: Illusion II

1 cup flour
2 tsp. baking powder
1/4 tsp. salt
2 Tblsp. cocoa
1/2 cup milk
1 cup nuts, chopped
1 cup brown sugar
1/4 cup cocoa
1-3/4 cup hot water
Garnish: whipped cream or vanilla ice cream

Preheat oven to 350 degrees F.
In a bowl blend first 6 ingredients and spread in a 9-inch pan. In a bowl blend brown sugar and cocoa, sprinkle over batter mixture. Pour hot water over all and bake for 40-45 minutes. *Serve with whipped cream or vanilla ice cream.*

Great for chocolate lovers!

Instead of slowly stirring a pudding mixture, mix a small amount of milk with the pudding ingredients. Heat the rest of the milk in another saucepan to almost boiling. Add hot milk to the mixture, stirring constantly, then pour back into the hot pan. Stir a short time and presto, the pudding is thickened.

TROPICAL LEMON TOP PUDDING

Preparation time: 10 minutes   *Chef: Jan Robinson*
Cooking time: 35 minutes   *Yacht: Vanity*
Serves: 4

2 egg yolks, lightly beaten
1 Tblsp. butter, softened
1/3 cup honey
1-1/2 Tblsp. whole wheat flour
1/4 cup lemon juice
1 cup milk
2 egg whites, beaten stiff

Preheat oven to 350 degrees F.
In a bowl mix egg yolks, butter and honey. Stir in flour, then add lemon juice and milk. Fold in egg whites. Pour into 4 ungreased individual custard cups. Place cups in a baking pan, pour hot water into pan around the cups, about halfway up the sides of cups. *Bake and serve.*

WEST INDIAN PUDDING

Preparation time: 10 minutes   *Chef: Jan Robinson*
Cooking time: 1 hour 10 minutes   *Yacht:Vanity*
Serves: 6

3 cups milk
1/2 cup molasses
1/3 cup yellow cornmeal
1/2 tsp. each of ground ginger and cinnamon
1 Tblsp. butter or margarine

Preheat oven to 300 degrees F.
In a saucepan mix milk and molasses; stir in cornmeal, ginger, cinnamon and salt. Cook and stir about 10 minutes or until thick. Stir in butter. Turn into an ungreased 1-quart casserole. Bake uncovered about 1 hour in a pan of hot water.

OREGON SURPRISE

Preparation time: 30 minutes
Cooking time: 6 minutes
Chilling time: 3-4 hours
Serves: 12

Chef: Peyt Turner
Yacht: Summertime

1/2 cup margarine
1 cup flour
1 cup walnuts, chopped
1 (8 oz.) pkg. cream cheese
1-1/2 cup powdered sugar
2 cups whipping cream
1 large pkg. instant pistaschio pudding mix
3 cups milk
Vanilla to taste

Preheat oven to 350 degrees F.
Blend margarine, flour and walnuts together and press into a 9x13 inch baking pan. Bake about 6 minutes or until almost brown, let cool. Beat the cream cheese, 1 cup powdered sugar and 1 cup whipping cream together until thick and pour onto crust. Combine pistaschio pudding mix, milk and vanilla, beat until stiff. Let stand a few minutes, then pour over cream cheese layer. For the topping, combine 1 cup whipping cream and 1/2 cup powdered sugar, spread over pudding layer. Refrigerate until serving.

Hint: *I generally do the crust the night before and then the rest of it early in the day and it will be ready to serve in the evening. This is a really good recipe, chocolate and lemon instant pudding mix can be substituted.*

PUSSER'S PROFITEROLES

Preparation time: 30 minutes
Cooking time: 20 minutes
Serves: 6

Chef: Vanessa Owen
Yacht: Endless Summer II

Profiteroles:
   3 Tblsp. butter
   1 cup water
   1/3 cup plain flour
   2 eggs, beaten
   1 cup whipped cream
Sauce:
   ]2 Tblsp. butter
   1/2 cup Pusser's Rum
   1 cup (8 oz.) semi-sweet chocolate morsels

Preheat oven to 350 degrees F.
Profiteroles: Place butter and water in a saucepan and bring to a boil stirring rapidly. Add flour and beat well, let cool slightly then beat in eggs. Pipe walnut-sized blobs onto a greased tray and bake for 20 minutes. When done, make a small hole in each and pipe in whipped cream.

Sauce: Melt butter in a saucepan, add Pusser's Rum and boil for 2 minutes. Melt the chocolate in a double boiler (or microwave), add to butter mixture, simmer for 5 minutes. *To serve: put the profiteroles in dessert glasses and pour the hot sauce over each. Delicious!*

A very English dessert that goes down as a treat. For a great hot and cold combination, fill each profiterole with ice cream instead of whipped cream for extra special guests.

CARIBBEAN RUM TRIFLE

Preparation time: 20 minutes　　　*Chef: Vanessa Owen*
Cooling time: 1 hour　　　　　　*Yacht: Endless Summer II*
Cooking time: 10 minutes
Serves: 8

1 pound cake, small
Raspberries in syrup
1/2 cup rum
Brown sugar
1/2 cup almonds
1/2 cup flaked coconut
1 lb. seasonal fresh fruit (plantains, pears, apples,
**   pineapple, kiwifruit, etc.)**
4 cups custard*
1 cup cream
Garnish: whipped cream and grated chocolate

***Use Bird's custard, or 1 (3-3/4 oz.) pkg. of**
**   vanilla pudding**

Crumble pound cake into individual dessert bowls; add raspberries and rum; divide evenly between bowls. Leave for 1 hour or until cake absorbs liquid. Make pudding according to instructions. In each dish layer the sugar, almonds, coconut and fresh fruit in distinct layers. Top with a dollop of custard. Cool until custard is set. *Pipe with whipped cream and grated chocolate on top.*

Note: *A teaspoon of cinnamon and 1/2 teaspoon of fresh nutmeg can be added to custard just before pouring over fruit for a truly Caribbean flavor.*

ENGLISH TRIFLE

Preparation time: 20 minutes   *Chef: Jan Robinson*
Cooking time: 10 minutes   *Yacht: Vanity*
Serves: 6-8

3 or 4 firm bananas, peeled and sliced
2 cups fresh raspberries
2 cups fresh peaches, or strawberries
1/2 cup pecan pieces, or slivered almonds
1 (3-3/4 oz.) pkg. vanilla pudding
1 pound cake, sliced
2 ozs. brandy
Garnish: 1 cup heavy cream whipped with
   1 tsp. brandy, grated chocolate

Note: If fresh fruit is not available, use unsweetened
   frozen, defrosted and drained

Select a glass serving bowl, about 7 inches in diameter and 4 inches deep. Mix all fruits and nuts. Prepare vanilla pudding as directed on pudding package and let cool. Arrange a layer of pound cake slices in the bowl. Top with a layer of mixed fruits and nuts, and sprinkle with brandy. Continue in layers. Spread vanilla pudding evenly over top of trifle. Place in the refrigerator for 1 hour or more for flavors to mingle. *To serve: mound whipped cream over trifle, sprinkle with chocolate. Spoon down through trifle so that each serving consists of whipped cream, pudding, fruit and cake.*

Hint: *If time permits, place the fruit decoratively inside the bowl against the glass. Looks and tastes great!*

PASSION FRUIT TRIFLE

Preparation time: 30 minutes   *Chef: Penny Knowles*
Chillng time: 1 hour   *Yacht: Golden Skye*
Serves: 8

1 pound cake
Passion fruit nectar
4 cups custard*
1/2 cup whipping cream
Garnish: passion fruit pulp and kiwi slices

*Custard can be made with Bird's mix; make it thick.

Slice pound cake and line the base of a glass bowl. Pour in enough passion fruit nectar to moisten, but not saturate the cake. Pour custard on top and chill. Whip cream with a little passion fruit juice to give it taste. Cover the top of the trifle with whipped cream and use decorative piping at the edge. *Garnish with kiwi slices and passion fruit pulp.*

EXOTIC ANGEL PUDDING

Preparation time: 30 minutes　　　　*Chef: Jan Robinson*
Chilling time: 1-2 hours　　　　　　　*Yacht:Vanity*
Serves: 8

1 angel food cake
1/3 cup dry sherry
1 (11 oz.) can Mandarin oranges
1/4 cup slivered almonds, toasted
1 (3-3/4 oz.) pkg. Dream Whip
Garnish: Mandarin oranges

Cut cake into 1 inch cubes. Place cubes in 12x8x2-inch baking dish. Drizzle sherry evenly over cake. Drain oranges, reserving syrup and 1/4 cup oranges for garnish, arrange remainder over cake.　Sprinkle with toasted almonds. Prepare Dream Whip according to package directions, substituting reserved orange syrup for the water. Pour evenly over cake. Chill thoroughly, 1-2 hours. *Garnish with Mandarin oranges.*

APRICOT SAUCE

Preparation time: 3 minutes
Cooking time: 30 minutes
Chilling time: 30 minutes
Makes: 2 cups

Chef: Jan Robinson
Yacht: Vanity

3/4 cup diced, dried apricots,
 soaked overnight
1/3 cup honey
1-1/2 cups water or soaking
 juice from apricots

Cook apricots, honey and water in a heavy saucepan, over low heat for about 30 minutes. Cool slightly, then process in blender until smooth. If necessary add water or any fruit juice to obtain the right consistency. Cool completely, put into sealed container and store in refrigerator.

BERRY SAUCE

Preparation time: 5 minutes　　　*Chef: Jan Robinson*
Cooking time: 7 minutes　　　　　*Yacht: Vanity*
Chilling time: 30 minutes
Makes: 2 cups

2 (10 oz.) pkgs. frozen unsweetened berries
　(strawberries, raspberries, blueberries),
　or 3 cups fresh berries
2-3 Tblsp. honey or sugar
2 tsp. cornstarch
1/2 tsp. lemon juice (optional)

In a small saucepan, combine berries and honey. Stir over low heat until just below boiling. Dissolve cornstarch into water and add to berry-honey mixture, add lemon juice, if desired. Cook slowly until thick and smooth. Strain sauce through coarse sieve, cool, place in covered container and store in refrigerator.

Note: *The amount of sugar or honey used, depends on the sweetness of the fruit.*

CARAMEL SAUCE

Preparation time: 5 minutes   *Chef: Jan Robinson*
Cooking time: 15 minutes   *Yacht: Vanity*
Makes about 3 cups

1-1/4 cups brown sugar
2/3 cup corn syrup or maple syrup
1/4 cup boiling water
3/4 cup light cream
1/4 tsp. grated nutmeg
1 tsp. vanilla extract

In a saucepan stir brown sugar, corn or maple syrup and boiling water over low heat until sugar is dissolved. Add light cream and cook until smooth. Stir frequently. Remove from heat; add the nutmeg and vanilla. *Long cooking over low heat makes this sauce smooth and velvety.*

Note: *Great with steamed pudding, ice cream, or baked apples.*

Alternative: Pour one can sweetened condensed milk into top of double boiler and place over boiling water. Over low heat, simmer 1 to 1-1/2 hours or until thick and caramel colored. Remove from heat and beat until smooth with a little vanilla and nutmeg. *Yummy!*

CHOCOLATE SAUCE

Preparation time: 5 minutes   *Chef: Jan Robinson*
Cooking time: 15 minutes   *Yacht: Vanity*
Makes: 3 cups

4 oz. (4 squares) usweetened chocolate
2 Tblsp. butter
1 cup confectioners sugar, sifted
1 cup light cream
Pinch of salt
3 Tblsp. dark rum

Melt the chocolate and butter over low heat or in a microwave. Add sugar, cream and salt. Cook over low heat, stirring constantly, until sauce reaches boiling point. Cook for a few minutes longer over very low heat, then stir in the rum. Leave over heat for 1 minute longer. *Serve this sauce hot or cold.*

Variation: *To make* **Mocha Sauce,** *dissolve 2 tsp. instant coffee powder into 1 tsp. water, add with the cream.*

Note: *Serve this sauce hot over cold ice cream, poached pears, meringues or pound cake.*

When liquor or flavorings are added to cooked sauce, they should be added after the sauce has been removed from the heat or just before serving. This prevents dissipation of the flavoring essences.

CUSTARD SAUCE

Preparation time: 5 minutes   *Chef: Jan Robinson*
Cooking time: 8-10 minutes   *Yacht: Vanity*
Makes about 3 cups

2 cups light cream
1/4 cup sugar or honey
1/2 vanilla bean
1/2 cup cold milk
4 egg yolks
1 Tblsp. cornstarch
1/4 tsp. salt
2 Tblsp. butter

In a saucepan place the cream, sugar and vanilla bean. Heat slowly over low heat. Beat together the cold milk and egg yolks. Add cornstarch and salt. Pour milk mixture into the hot cream, beating as you pour, and continue to beat with a wire whisk until blended. Add butter. Continue to cook over low heat, stirring constantly until the mixture will coat a spoon.

If sauce is to be served hot, remove vanilla bean and serve at once. If sauce is to be served cold, remove vanilla bean after covered sauce has cooled.

Note: *This light, but rich custard sauce can be served hot or cold with fruits, cakes, puddings and souffles. As a variation, you can stir in coconut just before serving.*

GINGER SAUCE

Preparation time: 10 minutes   *Chef: Jan Robinson*
Cooking time: 40 minutes   *Yacht: Vanity*
Makes about 1-1/2 cups

1 cup ginger root, soaked overnight
3 cups water
1 cup honey
1 Tblsp. cornstarch
1 Tblsp. water

Scrape and dice ginger root into 1/8-inch cubes or slices. Place in saucepan, add water cover and cook slowly for about 30 minutes. Drain, saving one cup of liquid. Put back into the saucepan, add honey and the diced ginger root. Boil, covered for about 10 minutes, or until mixture becomes syrupy. Combine cornstarch and water and add slowly to the ginger syrup. Cook until thick and smooth. Cool. Store in tightly closed jar in refrigerator.

Note: *Ginger Sauce is very powerful! But it is tasty and adds an exotic flavor if used sparingly over vanilla ice cream, plain pudding or baked custard.*

Most sauces can be made in advance and stored in a covered jar in the refrigerator. If jars are not completely filled, turn them upside down—their contents will stay fresh for a much longer time.

RUM–RAISIN SAUCE

Preparation time: 10 minutes ·   *Chef: Jan Robinson*
Cooking time: none   *Yacht: Vanity*
Makes about 2 cups

6 Tblsp. light cream
3 Tblsp. light rum
1/2 cup soft butter
1/3 cup honey
1/2 cup golden raisins

Put cream, rum and butter into a blender, cover and process at medium speed until smooth. (At this point the mixture looks slightly curdled or separated, but don't be concerned, just continue blending.) Add honey, then process just until raisins are chopped fine, not pureed. *This sauce is excellent over vanilla ice cream, cake or pudding.*

FRIENDSHIP

Preparation time: none   *Chefs: All*
Cooking time: a little   *Yachts: All*
Serves: lots

Take some morning sunshine
Add a smile, some words too ...
Sprinkle in some happy hours,
It's not hard to do ...
Add a little thoughtfuiness
Stir just enough to blend
Serve it warm with loving hands
It is the making of a friend.

Notes

POTPOURRI

Notes

HOW TO USE INGREDIENTS

FLOUR

All-purpose flour is a blend of hard- and soft-wheat flours. The combination allows it to be used in all types of baked goods, as well as for thickening.

Bread flour is made mostly of hard wheat which has a high amount of protein to stablize the structure of the bread.

Cake flour is a flour made from a softer wheat. It is used for making tender, delicate cakes.

Other types of flour include whole wheat, rye, and buckwheat flours, which are used mainly for specialty breads.

Self-rising flour is an all-purpose flour that contains added leavening and salt. It may be substituted for all-purpose flour in quick bread recipes, but the salt, baking powder, and baking soda must be omitted.

THICKENERS

Flour (all-purpose) may be used to thicken gravies, sauces, and puddings. It gives them an opaque appearance.

Cornstarch is used to thicken sauces and puddings when a translucent product is desired. It's thickening power is about twice that of flour. Similar thickeners are: potato, starches, and arrowroot powder.

Tapioca may be used to thicken pie filings and puddings. It forms a lumpy, but clear, mixture. Pearl tapioca is a slow-cooking variety, while quick-cooking tapioca requires less soaking.

Eggs also may be used to thicken mixtures, as well as add richness.

SWEETENERS

Besides their primary function of adding flavor, sweeteners affect the tenderness of baked goods and the consistency of puddings and sauces.

Superfine sugar has smaller particles than granulated but larger than powdered sugar and has no starch added.

Granulated sugar is a basic sweetener made from sugar cane or sugar beets (both kinds are the same).

Powdered sugar or *confectioners' sugar* is granulated sugar crushed and screened till grains are tiny. Starch is then added to keep lumping to a minimum. It's designed for use in uncooked frostings or icings and to dust over baked products.

Brown sugar is a less refined form of granulated sugar. It derives a special flavor and moistness from the molasses that clings to the granules. Dark brown sugar has a stronger flavor than light. A granulated form is available, but it can't be substituted for regular brown sugar in baking because its moisture content is lower.

Honey is made by bees from the nectar of flowers. It is sweeter than sugar, and adds a characteristic flavor to foods.

Syrups include corn, cane, sorghum, molasses, maple and fruit-flavored types. Each adds its distinctive flavor to foods. They are used as toppings as well as recipe ingredients.

Artificial sweeteners sweeten foods without the use of natural sugars. They cannot be substituted for sugar in baked foods because they do not have the other properties of sugar.

LEAVENINGS

Leavenings are the ingredients that cause a baked food to rise in the oven or on the griddle. In some products, such as cream puffs and angel cakes, the water turning to steam and air expanding are sufficient to leaven the food. But most baked goods require additional leavening agents.

Baking soda reacts with the acid in food to form carbon dioxide gas. The soda and acid begin to react as soon as liquid is added, so a product containing soda should be baked immediately after it is mixed. Some acidic foods that help complete the reaction are vinegar, lemon juice, cream of tartar, buttermilk, sour milk, brown sugar, and molasses.

Baking powder is a combination of baking soda and an acidic ingredient. It does not produce its full amount of leavening till heated, so the unbaked product is more stable than with soda.

Eggs can be used as leaveners by whipping the yolks or whites before adding to recipes.

Yeast is a microscopic plant that produces carbon dioxide from starch or sugar when placed in suitable conditions for growth. It can be purchased in the active dry or compressed form.

DAIRY PRODUCTS

Homogenized whole milk is milk that has been processed so that the fat does not rise to the tip. The fat content is a least 3.25%.

Skim milk has most of its fat removed, so its fat content is less than 0.5%. *Low-fat milk* has a fat content of 0.5% to 2%.

Nonfat dry milk is milk with both fat and water removed. It is processed to mix easily with water.

Evaporated milk has 60% of the water removed, and is processed in cans.

Sweetened condensed milk is milk with about half the water removed and a large amount of sugar added, and is also processed in cans.

Buttermilk is the liquid left after the butter-making process. More widely sold is cultured buttermilk, a product made by adding a bacteria to skim milk. The two ar interchangeable.

Yogurt is a creamy product made by fermenting milk.

Whipping cream also may be called heavy cream or light whipping cream. It contains 30% to 40% fat, and is suitable for whipping. *Light cream* contains 10% to 30% fat and includes half-and-half. It adds richness to recipes. *Dairy sour cream* is a commercially cultured light cream used to add a tangy flavor and richness to food.

EGGS

Eggs can be used to thicken mixtures, aerate, bind ingredients, or form a structure in baked goods.

DESSERT PREPARATION TERMS

Aerate Increase volume by incorporating air.

Bake Cook by dry heat in an oven or oven-like appliance. Always bake a dish uncovered unless recipe specifies otherwise.

Baking Dish A glass or ceramic container used in an oven.

Batter A mixture of ingredients that can be poured or dropped from a spoon.

Beat Mix by stirring rapidly in a circular motion by hand or with electric or rotary beater to make it smooth.

Blanch Briefly boil or steam a food to prevent spoilage during freezing, or to loosen skins for peeling.

Blend Mix two or more ingredients together until smooth or until they combine to produce a uniform texture, color or flavor.

Boil Agitate a liquid with heat until bubbles rise to the surface and break. In a full rolling boil, bubbles form rapidly throughout the mixture.

Caramelize Cook sugar slowly over low heat till it melts and turns golden brown or to heat sweetened condensed milk until thick and caramel colored.

Chill Refrigerate to reduce temperature of a food.

Chop Cut into small pieces.

Combine Mix two or more ingredients until blended.

Cool Stand at room temperature to reduce the temperature of a food. When a recipe says, "cool quickly," the food should be refrigerated or set in a bowl of ice water to quickly reduce its temperature.

Core Remove the center part of a fruit (apples, pineapple, etc.)

Cream Beat with a spoon or electric mixer to make mixture light and fluffy.

Cube Cut into pieces that are the same size on each side. (1/2 in.)

Dice Cut into cubes that are 1/8 to 1/4 inch on each side.

Dissolve Stir a dry ingredient into a liquid until the dry ingredient is no longer visible.

Fold Incorporate a light, areated mixture into a heavier mixture with a lifting, circular motion, without deflating the lighter mixture.

Garnish Decorate a food, usually with a flavorsome or colorful food.

Gel Convert a liquid to a solid tyupically having a jelly-like consistency.

Glaze Brush mixture on a food to give a glossy appearance or a hard finish, usually adds flavor.

Grate Rub solid food (lemon or orange rind, chocolate etc.) across a grater to produce fine shreds, flakes or tiny particles.

Hull Remove the outer parts of nuts; to remove stems and inner hard core from berries.

Knead Work dough with the hands in a pressing, folding, and turning motion into amalleable mass.

Line Cover the inside or just the bottom of a pan with a piece of aluminum foil, wax paper or parchment paper.

Marinate Allow a food to stand in a liquid that adds flavor to the food.

Mix Combine ingredients by stirring.

Pan Metal container to which direct heat can be applied, on the stove top or in oven.

Partially set When a gelatin mixture reaches the consistency of raw egg whites.

Pit Remove the seed from a piece of fruit.

Pare/Peel Remove the rind or skin from fruit.

Poach Cook in hot liquid, making sure the food holds its shape.

Puree Blend, sieve or process into a soft, smooth consistency, either a liquid or heavy paste.

Reduce Boil rapidly to evaporate liquid so mixture becomes thicker.

Sauté Cook quickly in a small amount of butter, margarine, oil or shortening.

Scald Bring to a temperature just below boiling so that tiny bubbles form at the edges of pan.

Score Cut shallow grooves or slits through the outer layer of a food.

Sift Pass flour or a dry mixture through a sieve or sifter to incorporate air, mix and break up lumps.

Simmer Cook in liquid just below the boiling point.

Sprinkle Scatter small particles or drops on top of food.

Steep Extract the flavor or color from a substance by letting it stand in hot liquid.

Stir Mix ingredients together with a spoon until well blended using a slow, wide, circular motion; do not beat.

Toast Toast nuts or coconut by baking in oven until light golden brown (or until nuts are crisp and dry).

Toss Mix ingredients lightly by lifting and dropping with a spoon, or a spoon and fork.

Turn out Remove a baked product from the pan in which it was baked.

Whip Beat lightly and rapidly, in a cicular motion, incorporating air into a mixture to make it light and to increase its volume.

EQUIVALENT CHART

When the recipe calls for:	Use:
B **A** **K** **I** **N** **G** **E** **S** **S** **E** **N** **T** **I** **A** **L** **S**	1/2 cup butter — 1 stick 2 cups butter — 1 pound 4 cups all-purpose flour — 1 pound 4-1/2 - 5 cups sifted cake flour — 1 pound 1 square chocolate — 1 ounce 1 cup semi-sweet chocolate pieces — 1 - 6 ounce package 4 cups marshmallows — 1 pound 8 large marshmallows — 1 cup miniature marshmallows 2-1/4 cups packed brown sugar — 1 pound 4 cups confectioners' sugar — 1 pound 2 cups granulated sugar — 1 pound 18 graham cracker squares — 1-1/4 cups crumbs 12 chocolate sandwich cookies — 1 cup crumbs 20 chocolate wafer cookies — 1 cup crumbs 24 vanilla wafers — 1 cup crumbds 18 ginger snaps — 1 cup crumbs

	When the recipe calls for:	Use:
B A K I N G **E S S E N T I A L S**	1/2 cup butter	1 stick
	2 cups butter	1 pound
	4 cups all-purpose flour	1 pound
	4-1/2 - 5 cups sifted cake flour	1 pound
	1 square chocolate	1 ounce
	1 cup semi-sweet chocolate pieces	1 - 6 ounce package
	4 cups marshmallows	1 pound
	8 large marshmallows	1 cup miniature marshmallows
	2-1/4 cups packed brown sugar	1 pound
	4 cups confectioners' sugar	1 pound
	2 cups granulated sugar	1 pound
	18 graham cracker squares	1-1/4 cups crumbs
	12 chocolate sandwich cookies	1 cup crumbs
	20 chocolate wafer cookies	1 cup crumbs
	24 vanilla wafers	1 cup crumbds
	18 ginger snaps	1 cup crumbs
D A I R Y	1 large egg	3 Tblsp. egg
	1 large egg white	2 Tblsp. white
	1 large egg yolk	1 Tblsp. yolk
	1 cup sour cream	1 - 8 ounce carton
	1 cup whipped cream	1/2 cup heavy cream
	2/3 cup evaporated milk	1 small can
	1-2/3 cups evaporated milk	1 - 13 ounce can
F R U I T	4 cups sliced or chopped apples	4 medium
	1 cup mashed banana	3 medium
	2 cups pitted cherries	4 cups unpitted
	3 cups shredded coconut	1/2 pound
	4 cups cranberries	1 pound
	1 cup pitted dates	1 - 8 ounce package
	1 cup candied fruit	1 - 8 ounce package
	3 - 4 Tblsp. lemon juice plus 1 tsp. grated rind	1 lemon
	1/3 cup orange juice plus 2 tsp. grated rind	1 orange
	4 cups sliced peaches	8 medium
	2 cups pitted prunes	1 - 12 ounce package
	3 cups raisins	1 - 15 ounce package
N U T S	1 cup chopped nuts	4 ounces shelled *or* 1 pound unshelled

FREEZER STORAGE FOR DESSERTS

Cakes	Any type butter cake* Frosted or unfrosted ....4–6 mos. Angelfood or Chiffon.......................2 mos. Fruit .... 12 mos.
Cookies	Baked..6–8 mos. Unbaked ....6 mos.
Dairy **Products**	Butter...6 mos. Margarine .... 12 mos. Cream Cheese ....2 mos. Cream, heavy ....0 mos. (may not whip after freezing) Half n' Half ....2 mos. Whipped Cream .... 1 mo. Eggs - whole or separated............. 12 mos.
Desserts	Cream Puffs or Eclairs .... 1–2 mos. Fruit...2–4 mos. Ice cream, Sherbert, etc..................6 mos.
Nuts	Unsalted ....9–12 mos. Salted ....6–8 mos.
Pastries	Pastry dough Unbaked........................... 1-1/2–2 mos. Baked ....6–8 mos. Pies* Unbaked ....2–4 mos. Baked ....6–8 mos. Chiffon ....2 mos.

*Do not freeze cakes or pies filled with
custard or cream or meringues

PAN AND BAKING DISH SIZES

4-CUP BAKING DISH=	9" pie plate 8" layer cake pan 7-3/8 x 3-5/8" loaf pan
6-CUP BAKING DISH=	8 or 9" layer cake pan 10" pie plate 8-1/2 x 3-5/8" loaf pan
8-CUP BAKING DISH=	8 x 8"square pan 11 x 7" baking pan 9 x 5" loaf pan
10-CUP BAKING DISH=	9 x 9" square pan 11-3/4 x 7-1/2" baking pan 15 x 10" jelly roll pan
12-CUP BAKING DISH AND OVER	13-1/2 x 8-1/2" glass baking pan = 12 cups 13 x 9" metal baking pan = 15 cups 14 x 10-1/2" roasting pan = 19 cups

VOLUME OF SPECIAL BAKING PANS

TUBE PANS	CUPS	SPRINGFORM PANS	CUPS
7-1/2 x 3" bundt pan	6	8 x 3" pan	12
9 x 3-1/2" bundt pan	9	9 x 3" pan	16
9 x 3-1/2" angel cake	12		
10 x 3/4" bundt pan	12	RING MOLDS	CUPS
10 x 4" angel cake pan	18	8-1/2 x 2-1/4"	4-1/2

MOLDS	CUPS	BRIOCHE PAN	CUPS
7 x 5-1/2 x 4" mold	6	9-1/2 x 3-1/4" pan	8

EMERGENCY SUBSTITUTIONS

For best results, use ingredients specified in the recipes since substitutions often change the flavor and texture. But when you're caught between the Devil and the deep blue sea, use this chart to find an acceptable substitute.

If You Don't Have:	Substitute:
1 cup of cake flour	1 cup minus 2 Tblsp. all-purpose flour
1 tablespoon cornstarch	2 Tblsp. all-purpose flour *or* 1 Tblsp. tapioca
1 teaspoon baking powder	1/4 tsp. baking soda plus 1/2 tsp. cream of tartar
1 cup granulated sugar	1 cup packed brown sugar *or* 2 cups sifted powdered sugar
1 cup honey	1-1/4 cups granulated sugar plus 1/4 cup liquid *or* 1 cup corn syrup
1 cup corn syrup	1 cup granulated sugar plus 1/4 cup liquid
1 square unsweetened chocolate (1 oz.)	3 Tblsp. unsweetened cocoa powder plus 1 Tblsp. butter or margarine
1 cup sour milk or buttermilk	1 Tblsp. lemon juice or vinegar plus whole milk to make 1 cup (let stand 5 minutes before using) *or* 1 cup whole milk plus 1-3/4 tsp. cream of tartar *or* 1 cup plain yogurt
1 cup sour cream	7/8 cup sour milk plus 3 Tblsp. butter

If You Don't Have:	Substitute:
1 cup whole milk	1/2 cup evaporated milk plus 1/2 cup water *or* 1 cup reconstituted non-fat dry milk plus 2 tsp. butter or margarine
1 cup light cream	2 Tblsp. butter plus 1 cup minus 2 Tblsp. milk
1 tsp. lemon peel finely grated	1/2 tsp. lemon extract
1 whole egg	2 egg yolks (for most uses)

MICROWAVE TIPS

SOFTENING:

Ingredient	Power Level	Time
1/2 cup margarine or butter	30% power (med.-low)	30 - 50 seconds
3 oz. cream cheese	50% power (med.)	30 - 60 seconds
8 oz. cream cheese	50% power (med.)	1 to 1-1/2 min.

MELTING:

1/4 cup margarine or butter	100% power (high)	45 - 60 seconds
1/2 cup margarine or butter	100% power (high)	45 - 90 seconds
1 cup margarine or butter	100% power (high)	1 - 2 min.
1 cup chocolate chips	50% power (med.)	2-1/2-3-1/2 min.
2 squares baking chocolate	50% power (med.)	2-1/2-3-1/2 min.
4 squares baking chocolate	50% power (med.)	2-1/2-4 min.
4 oz. sweet chocolate	50% power (med.)	2-1/2-4 min.
1 pound candy coating	50% power (med.)	3 - 5 min.

Coconut: spread 1/2 cup coconut in glass pie plate. Cook on 70% power (med.-high) 5 to 10 minutes or until lightly browned, stirring after each minute.

Nuts: Spread 1 cup nuts in glass pie plate. Cook on 100% power (high) 5 to 8 minutes or until lightly browned, stirring after each minute. In a microwave oven nuts heat quickly and brown evenly. Remove from oven as soon as they *begin* to brown (browning will continue as they stand).

APPROXIMATE TEMPERATURE CONVERSIONS
FAHRENHEIT TO CELSIUS

	FAHRENHEIT (°F)	CELSIUS (°C)
FREEZER		
Coldest area	-10°	-23°
Overall	0°	-17°
WATER		
Freezes	32°	0°
Simmers	115°	46°
Scalds	130°	55°
Boils (sea level)	212°	100°
OVEN		
Slow	250°–325°	121°–163°
Moderate	325°–375°	163°–191°
Moderate - Hot	375°–400°	191°–204°
Hot	400°–450°	204°–232°

Fahrenheit to Celsius: Subtract 32-Multiply by 5-Divide by 9. (°F-32x5÷9=°C)
Celsius to Fahrenheit: Multiply by 9-Divide by 5-Add 32. (°Cx9÷5+32=°F)

TEMPERATURE CONVERSION
FROM FAHRENHEIT TO CELSIUS*

Fahrenheit	200	225	250	275	300	325	350
Celsius	93	106	121	135	149	163	176
Fahrenheit	375	400	425	450	475	500	550
Celsius	191	204	218	232	246	260	288

TEMPERATURE CONVERSIONS FOR CANDY

Cold Water Test	Fahrenheit °F	Celsius °C
Thread: Syrup dropped from spoon spins 2-inch thread.	230°–234°	110°–112°
Soft-ball: Syrup can be shaped into a ball that flattens when removed from water.	234°–240°	112°–116°
Firm-Ball: Syrup can be shaped into a firm ball that does not flatten when removed from water.	244°–248°	118°–120°
Hard-ball: Syrup forms a hard ball that is pliable.	250°–266°	121°–130°
Soft-crack: Syrup separates into threads that are not brittle.	270°–290°	132°–143°
Hard-crack: Syrup separates into hard, brittle threads.	300°–310°	149°–154°

TABLE OF MEASUREMENTS AND EQUIVALENTS
U. S. AND METRIC

U. S.	EQUIVALENTS	METRIC *Volume - Milliliters*
Dash	Less than 1/8 teaspoon	5 ml.
1 teaspoon	60 drops	15 ml.
1 Tablespoons	3 teaspoons	30 ml.
2 Tablespoons	1 fluid ounce	60 ml.
4 Tablespoons	1/4 cup or 2 fluid ounces	80 ml.
5-1/3 Tablespoons	1/3 cup	90 ml.
6 Tablespoons	3/8 cup	120 ml.
8 Tablespoons	1/2 cup or 4 fluid ounces	160 ml.
10-2/3 Tablespoons	2/3 cup	180 ml.
12 Tablespoons	3/4 cup or 6 fluid ounces	240 ml.
16 Tablespoons	1 cup or 8 ounces	240 ml.
1 cup	1/2 pint or 8 fluid ounces	480 ml.
2 cups	1 pint	480 ml. or .473 liter
1 pint	16 ounces	960 ml. or .95 liter
1 quart	2 pints	1 liter
2.1 pints	1.05 quarts or .26 gallon	1.9 liters
2 quarts	1/2 gallon	3.8 liters
4 quart	1 gallon	

Weight - Grams

1 ounce	16 drams	28 grams
1 pound	16 ounces	454 grams
1 pound	16 ounces	454 grams
2.20 pounds	35.2 ounces	1 kilogram

COOKING MEASURE EQUIVALENTS

U. S. CUP	VOLUME (Liquid)	LIQUID SOLIDS (Butter)	FINE POWDER (Flour)	GRANULAR (Sugar)	GRAIN (Rice)
1	250 ml	200 g	140 g	190 g	150 g
3/4	188 ml	150 g	105 g	143 g	113 g
2/3	167 ml	133 g	93 g	127 g	100 g
1/2	125 ml	100 g	70 g	95 g	75 g
1/3	83 ml	67 g	47 g	63 g	50 g
1/4	63 ml	50 g	35 g	48 g	38 g
1/8	31 ml	25 g	18 g	24 g	19 g

INDEX

Notes

PARTICIPATING YACHTS

PARTICIPATING YACHTS

Alizé: *Captain Guy Pyck, Chef Kate Young*
Not just another charter yacht! She's a 55' cutter, fast, spacious and comfortable. Enjoy fine cuisine, a multitude of watersports and lots of fun in the sun. Kate and Guy, a fun loving couple, welcome you to share this paradise. Won't you join us?

Ambience: *Captain Sharee Winslow, Chef Sande Buxton*
Enjoy the *Ambience* luxuriously appointed 51' ketch with all the amenities and water toys needed for your enjoyment. Cruising the Caribbean year round, come enjoy the *Ambience* of it all.

Annie Laurie: *Captain Jim MacDougall, Chef Karen Ciminelli*
Annie Laurie is a 49' Hinckley, a true luxury, world class sailing yacht with accommodations for four guests. Owner and Captain Jim has used her for chartering in the Virgin Islands and Caribbean since 1985. Jim and Karen are easy going, fun loving people, who will make your charter "A Vacation of a Lifetime!"

Ann-Marie II: *Captain Ken Haworth, Chef Margot Drybrough*
Ann-Marie II, a 38' classic all steel Zeeland yawl, was built 34 years ago; a sailboat unsurpassed in beauty and craftsmanship. Her interior of stained-glass and mahogany gives a warm feeling of old world charm. Ken and Margo take a maximum of two guests per charter, on a vacation you'll always remember.

Antiquity: *Captain David De Cuir, Chef Suzanne R. Copley*

Apjac: *Captain David Riel, Chef Carole Borden*

Aquarius: *Captain John Borden, Chef Wendy Riel*
Join John and Carole aboard *Aquarius*, a French designed racing sloop which provides all the amenities at one of the most affordable prices in the Caribbean.

Capricious: *Captain Cameron Hilton, Chef Kelly Reed*
Capricious is a 48' Sparkman and Stephens ketch with three double cabins finished in traditional teak and mahogany. The open and airy main salon, combined with both classic and innovative menus provide casual elegance at its best.

Cerulean: *Captain Michael Pavelka, Chef Debbie Rae*
Aboard the motoryacht *Cerulean*, meals are a very important part of the charter experience. Gourmet fare, breakfast, lunch and dinner keeps meal time exciting. Special occasions are celebrated in high spirit and exotic drinks can always be whipped up for blender sports! Bon Appetit and Bon Voyage!

Chardonnay: *Captain William C. Hadley, Chef Paulette Cook Hadley*
Bill and Paulette own and operate a superbly maintained and luxurious cutter/ketch that is well known for its warmth and relaxed environment. *Chardonnay* accommodates up to two couples in total comfort. They tailor their menus and activities so you leave as friends who just had their vacation fantasies realized.

Covenant II: *Captain Walter Matheson, Chef Gina Stafford*
Covenant II, a 53' Pearson ketch, charters in the Caribbean in the winter and spends the summer in Beaufort, N.C. She is a fast, luxurious, clean sailing yacht with a professional crew whose prime objective is to make your vacation one of a kind! Come sail with us!

Dileas: *Captain Dave Crook, Chef Jean Crook*
Dileas is a 60' Gulfstar. A very comfortable charter boat and a very nice, stiff sailing vessel. We are still in the charter business because we enjoy people of all walks of life.

Empress: *Captain Peter Polen, Chef Ramona Polen*
A luxurious 42' motoryacht, superbly decorated. accommodates four guests and two crew. *Empress* spends her summers cruising the Inland Waterways of Pennsylvania and winters Bluewater Voyaging out of West Palm Beach, Florida. The Captain proudly displays his International mermaid collection to all those welcomed aboard.

Encore: *Captain Allen Glen, Chef Vivian Phelps*
A 52' Trimaran provides spaciousness for up to eight guests. Windsurf, mini-sail, dive and water-ski. Owner/operated–split season for crews: Allen Glenn and Vivian Phelps from November 1st - May 1st; Marvin and Ann Phelps from May 1st - November 1st. "Scrumptious food."

Endless Summer II: *Captain Barry Rice, Chef Vanessa Owen*
Endless Summer II is a yacht and crew that offers:
Endless fun
Endless sun
Endless laughing
Endless diving
Endless beaches
Endless sailing
Endless gourmet dining
Endless memories
Endless summer.

Endless Summer 48: *Captain Martin Thomas, Chef Judy Knape*
Endless Summer 48 is a 48' custom sloop which carries two to four guests. Ideal for honeymooners. She has a spacious airy aft master stateroom with en suite head and cedar closet, as well as a comfortable forward cabin. Her crew has over ten years experience throughout the Caribbean and looks forward to showing guests the joys of sailing our pristine seas.

Freight Train II: *Captain George Banker, Chef Candice Carson*
A boat who sails as fast as her name.
Operated by owners in the charter game.
Escape the cold, the frazzles, and the mundane.
Let your body grow healthy, your mind grow sane.
If you have gotten this far, you know poets we're not.
But good cooks and fun people reside on this yacht.

Golden Skye: *Captain Gary Knowles, Chef Penny Knowles*
Golden Skye is a 63' custom ketch made specifically for luxury chartering. Owner/operators Penny and Gary Knowles offer exceptional elegance and superb cuisine. Golden Skye is a floating island where life is gracious, where every room overlooks the ocean and where dreams really do come true.

Gypsy: *Captain Glen Allen, Chef Suzan Salisbury*
Fun, lots of deck space, lots of toys and great food. A custom 65' ketch with four private double cabins. USCG certification. Ideal sailing yacht for young and old, family reunions and fun get togethers.

Gypsy Wind: *Captain Clive Petrovic, Chef Amanda Baker*
A customized 46' Morgan catering primarily to couples. Ideal for honeymoons. Full scuba gear including tanks and compressor. Captain is a scuba instructor. Diving available from beginning snorkeling to most advanced divers. Underwater cameras, onboard aquarium and tons of toys.

Hiya: *Captain Andy Smith, Chef Wendy Smith*
Wendy and Andy divide their time between chartering in the Caribbean and tending to their tree farm in Pennsylvania. They look forward to welcoming you aboard

Icebear: *Captain Bob Befield, Chef Laura Flintoff, Mate Jan Martin*

Illusion II: *Captain Roger Perkins, Chef Ronnie Hochman*
Illusion II is a flush deck, custom 55' ketch. Three double staterooms can accommodate up to six guests. Diving and windsurfing gear are aboard.

Iona of the Islands: *Captain Dan Cunningham, Chef Ninia Cunningham*
Conceived specially for charter, *Iona of the Islands* is the forerunner of the 1990's new generation of yachts. It offers you the ultimate in luxury and comfort afloat, while being pampered by a professional team which has a decade and a half of experience in the Virgin Islands.

Jewell: *Captain Jim Frey, Chef Connie Frey*
Jewell, a 66' motoryacht, with owner/operators Jim and Connie Frey aboard offers casual luxury for up to six guests in three private staterooms, each with ensuite full bath. Full line of water toys available with crew of three to teach and pamper guests. In the Virgin Islands year round.

KEA I: *Captain Lucren Schiltz, Chef Szilvia Schiltz*

Lady Privilege: *Captain Hugh R. Callum, Chef Cathleen H. Govatski*
Lady Privilege is a 48' Jeantot catamaran built in France. She carries six charter guests. The atmosphere is formal yet fun.

Marantha: *Captain Rob Fortune, Chef Gretchen Fater*
Marantha is a 62' ketch offering charters in New England and the Caribbean. Designed by the Captain for openness and space. Spacious main salon feels like a living room at sea. Please join us.

Ocean Voyager: *Captain Martin Vanderwood, Chef Marion Vanderwood*
Ocean Voyager is a 60' modern schooner. Martin and Marion Vanderwood, her dependable crew, welcome you to join them for the vacation of a lifetime. From the culinary delights from her galley to her superb sailing performance, it is where you want to be!

Perfection: *Captain Skip Lookabaugh, Chef Beth Avore*
Perfection is a Gulfstar 60' sloop. The first Mark II and Gulfstars show boat in 1986. With her roomy salon, deluxe master stateroom, two forward cabins and spacious cockpit, she's perfect for a leisurely cruise through the Virgins or a down-island charter, while providing the comforts of home.

Pride of Lyn: *Captain Jim Allen, Chef Allison Moir*
Pride of Lyn is a Nautical 60' ketch. She offers spacious accommodations for six guests in three double staterooms, with delicious meals, a friendly atmosphere and large open decks for fun and relaxation. Let Jim and Allison "sail your cares away!"

Promenade: *Captain David Dugdale, Chef Fiona Dugdale*
Your hosts Fiona and David bring to you the dedication that only owner/operators have. Fiona's Cordon Bleu cuisine and David's underwater sports, including scuba, and the simple pleasures of relaxing on her huge deck area make *Promenade* the yacht for the vacation you'll keep coming back to.

Qúe Sera: *Captain Rodney Davis, Chef Sharon Davis*
Qúe Sera, a 46' Celestial ketch, beautifully appointed with customized teak interior, she takes two to four guests with maximum comfort. Her crew will provide you with the ultimate sailing vacation.

Rhapsody: *Captain Bruce Dawes, Chef Aija Eglité*
Flavor your vacation with fast sailing, fantastic food and a fun loving crew on board *Rhapsody*. 72 feet of performance without compromising comfort. Daylight come, you NO wanna go home!

Rising Sun 64: *Captain Trevor Kehl, Chef Karen Roest*
Rising Sun 64 is a sleek, blue hulled, custom built schooner. She and her crew have had three successful seasons in the Virgin Islands and look forward to more!

Sabina D: *Captain Peo Stenberg, Chef Marilyn Stenberg*
To sail a Swan is to indulge in one of sporting's greatest privileges; to charter the Swan 65, *Sabina D*, is to create your own personal adventure–your own private pleasure. Peo and Marilyn will insure the cruise for a life-time and tempt you with many dishes from their truly international repertoire.

Scarlet Rose: *Captain Richard Owen, Chef Vanessa Owen*
Scarlet Rose is our dream, a little red ship that is carrying us around the world in faltering steps. Our guests, our friends join us from time to time, to keep this dream alive.

Serenity: *Captain Ray Zanusso, Chef Joanne Zanusso*

Silver Spirit: *Captain Steve Imbrogno, Chef Emily Imbrogno*
Silver Spirit is a fast and spacious Beneteau 51' sloop chartered by The Moorings, Ltd., Crewed Yacht Division. Her three equal staterooms, gourmet dining and lively sailing make for an unforgettable vacation for up to six guests.

Sloopy: *Captain Ed Doll, Chef Judy Garry*

Sly Mongoose: *Captain Rob Hancock, Chef Anna Hancock*
Sly Mongoose is a 54' custom aluminum cutter, originally designed to race the I. O. R. circuit, she has recently been refitted with all the charter amenities. Rob from New England and Anna from Milano, Italy, are now chartering in the Virgin Islands.

Solid Gold, Too: *Captain Steve Muse, Chef John Freeman*
British-born John Freeman was trained and gained experience in fine restaurants and hotels in and around his hometown of Stratford-on-Avon. For the past several years he has been tempting the palates of guests aboard yachts sailing the Caribbean. He is currently the chef on Solid Gold, Too, an 82-foot twin-engine Huckins, skippered by Captain Steve Muse and headquartered in St. Thomas and the Bahamas.

Southern Cruz: *Captain Scott Vallerga, Chef Christy Clifford*
Southern Cruz is a 68' Sparkman and Stephens ketch chartering the Virgin Islands and New England areas. Experienced crew and dive instructors, lots of sailing, water sports, good food and good times.

Stowaway: *Captain Jan Andersen, Chef Jolyne Grondin*
Stowaway Gulfstar sloop. LOA 50', beam 13'8", roller furling stowaway main, 85 hp. engine, 2 generators, 310 gallon water storage, 50 gallons fuel, center cockpit, NAV equipment, SAT-NAV, radar, Loran, VHF, liferaft, cellular phone, recreation windsurfer, dinghy with outboard, snorkeling gear, deck shower, 35mm underwater camera, 2 color TVs, VCR, deck speakers, stereo cassette and CD, AC, BBQ, hammock, cockpit dining, sailing bimini. Sail the Caribbean and New England.

Summertime: *Captain Bill Irwin, Chef Peyt Turner*

Tranquility: *Captain William Gibson, Chef Liz Thomas-Gibson*
Tranquility is a custom Tayana 55, built for comfort matched with performance sailing. Captains Bil and Liz Gibson have been chartering for eight years together, with four years on Tranquility. From the exciting sailing to the scrumptious meals Liz serves on board, we'll show you a vacation you'll never forget.

Traveline: *Captain Charles Curren, Chef Peggy Curren*
Traveline is a 76' custom built cutter-rigged motorsailer. She takes two couples or a family of six in two private cabins. Enjoy her spacious teak decks or her cool contemporary interior. She's sleek and sumptuous–a head-turner both from outwards to within. Let Charles and Peggy treat you to the vacation you've been waiting for!

Tri "My Way": *Captain Phil May, Chef Nancy May*
My Way is a 60' trimaran that accommodates 6-10 guests. There are 5 queen-size berths. My Way is very spacious. My Way offers scuba diving along with many other activities. Nancy and Phil May are enthusiastic to share their love for the islands.

Tri-World: *Captain James Eldridge, Chef Kate Chivas*
Tri-World, a 58' trimaran, welcomes you to a Virgin Islands vacation filled with diving, sailing, swimming, snorkeling, windsurfing, water-skiing, beach combing or just relaxing. Our yacht has three spacious guest cabins with private head and shower. Kate has been chef on Tri-World for two years. She's worked in many local restaurants on Cape Cod.

Vanity: *Captains Bob and Jan Robinson, Chef Jan Robinson*
Vanity, a luxurious 60' motorsailer. This owner/operated charter yacht is designed for privacy. Taking only four guests, Vanity assures you of individual consideration. Dine comfortably under the stars, enjoy international cuisine. Twelve years of chartering give the Robinsons the knowledge of where the action is and where serenity prevails.

Verano Sin Final: *Captain Frank Holden, Chef Shirley Benjamin*
Experience paradise on *Verano Sin Final.* Sail in style with your own professional crew, chosen for their ability to serve you and to handle *Verano* and her equipment. You will find us friendly, interesting and either active participants or attentive bystanders while you water-ski, snorkel, dive, explore and enjoy our gourmet meals.

Victorious: *Captain Thomas Boyce, Chef Sheila Kruse Boyce*
A delightful blend of modern (Hood stowaway masts, microwave, air conditioning, all the watersport toys) and traditional (beautiful teak interior, schooner rig). This 62' bluewater sailor caters to total luxury. Your crew will see that all your sailing fantasies come true, with their rich knowledge of the entire Caribbean—its wonderful sights and gourmet cuisine.

Voila: *Captain Greg Geelhood, Chef Lindsay Geelhood*
Wind Gypsy: *Captain Kevin Foley, Chef Nancy Drual*

ABOUT THE ARTIST

Our ingenious illustrator/artist, Raid (ray-eed) Ahmad, is part of the **Ship To Shore** success with **Sweet To Shore** being his latest.

He works with major publishers, newpapers and magazines. His illustrations are found in various publications including *Cats Magazine.* Raid has participated in many international exhibitions for which he has won numerous awards.

Cruise through our sweet temptations with Ahmad's cartoon characters and their sweet ideas!

SHIP TO SHORE, INC.

10500 MT. HOLLY ROAD
CHARLOTTE, NC 28214-9347

FREE !!!

Share the taste of the Caribbean with your friends !

We will send your friends a FREE catalog. Simply mail this form or call 1-800-338-6072

Name_____   Name_____

Address_____   Address_____

City_____   City_____

State_____Zip_____   State_____Zip_____

PERFECT GIFTS FOR ANY OCCASION

-- -- -- -- -- -- -- -- -- -- -- -- -- -- -- -- -- -- -- --

SHIP TO SHORE, INC.

10500 MT. HOLLY ROAD
CHARLOTTE, NC 28214-9347

FREE !!!

Share the taste of the Caribbean with your friends !

We will send your friends a FREE catalog. Simply mail this form or call 1-800-338-6072

Name_____   Name_____

Address_____   Address_____

City_____   City_____

State_____Zip_____   State_____Zip_____

PERFECT GIFTS FOR ANY OCCASION

RE-ORDER ADDITIONAL COPIES

AUTOGRAPH TO:

Qua.	Description	Price	Total
	SHIP TO SHORE I	$14.95	
	SHIP TO SHORE II	$14.95	
	SWEET TO SHORE	$14.95	
	SEA TO SHORE	$14.95	
	SIP TO SHORE	$10.95	

SHIP TO:

SHIP TO SHORE
10500 Mount Holly Road
Charlotte, NC 28214-9347
(704) 392-4740

5% Tax (NC only)	
Gift Wrap $1.00 Ea.	
Freight $1.50 Per/Bk	
TOTAL	

AUTOGRAPH TO:

SHIP TO:

Please charge my: MASTERCARD ☐   VISA ☐
AM EX ☐   CHECK ☐   MONEY ORDER ☐
Payable to: SHIP TO SHORE, INC.

MY CREDIT CARD NUMBER IS:

CALL TO ORDER TOLL FREE
1-800-338-6072

Signature:_____   Exp. Date: ☐☐☐☐

RE-ORDER ADDITIONAL COPIES

AUTOGRAPH TO:

Qua.	Description	Price	Total
	SHIP TO SHORE I	$14.95	
	SHIP TO SHORE II	$14.95	
	SWEET TO SHORE	$14.95	
	SEA TO SHORE	$14.95	
	SIP TO SHORE	$10.95	

SHIP TO:

SHIP TO SHORE
10500 Mount Holly Road
Charlotte, NC 28214-9347
(704) 392-4740

5% Tax (NC only)	
Gift Wrap $1.00 Ea.	
Freight $1.50 Per/Bk	
TOTAL	

AUTOGRAPH TO:

SHIP TO:

Please charge my: MASTERCARD ☐   VISA ☐
AM EX ☐   CHECK ☐   MONEY ORDER ☐
Payable to: SHIP TO SHORE, INC.

MY CREDIT CARD NUMBER IS:

CALL TO ORDER TOLL FREE
1-800-338-6072

Signature:_____   Exp. Date: ☐☐☐☐

RE-ORDER ADDITIONAL COPIES

AUTOGRAPH TO:

Qua.	Description	Price	Total
	SHIP TO SHORE I	$14.95	
	SHIP TO SHORE II	$14.95	
	SWEET TO SHORE	$14.95	
	SEA TO SHORE	$14.95	
	SIP TO SHORE	$10.95	

SHIP TO:

SHIP TO SHORE
10500 Mount Holly Road
Charlotte, NC 28214-9347
(704) 392-4740

6% Tax (NC only)

Gift Wrap $1.00 Ea.

Freight $1.50 Per/Bk

TOTAL

AUTOGRAPH TO:

SHIP TO:

Please charge my: MASTERCARD ☐   VISA ☐
AM EX ☐   CHECK ☐   MONEY ORDER ☐
Payable to: SHIP TO SHORE, INC.
MY CREDIT CARD NUMBER IS:

CALL TO ORDER TOLL FREE
1-800-338-6072

Signature: _____ Exp. Date: ☐☐☐☐

- -

RE-ORDER ADDITIONAL COPIES

AUTOGRAPH TO:

Qua.	Description	Price	Total
	SHIP TO SHORE I	$14.95	
	SHIP TO SHORE II	$14.95	
	SWEET TO SHORE	$14.95	
	SEA TO SHORE	$14.95	
	SIP TO SHORE	$10.95	

SHIP TO:

SHIP TO SHORE
10500 Mount Holly Road
Charlotte, NC 28214-9347
(704) 392-4740

6% Tax (NC only)

Gift Wrap $1.00 Ea.

Freight $1.50 Per/Bk

TOTAL

AUTOGRAPH TO:

SHIP TO:

Please charge my: MASTERCARD ☐   VISA ☐
AM EX ☐   CHECK ☐   MONEY ORDER ☐
Payable to: SHIP TO SHORE, INC.
MY CREDIT CARD NUMBER IS:

CALL TO ORDER TOLL FREE
1-800-338-6072

Signature: _____ Exp. Date: ☐☐☐☐

SHIP TO SHORE, INC.

10500 MT. HOLLY ROAD
CHARLOTTE, NC 28214-9347

FREE !!!

Share the taste of the Caribbean with your friends !

We will send your friends a FREE catalog. Simply mail this form or call 1-800-338-6072

Name_____   Name_____

Address_____   Address_____

City_____   City_____

State_____Zip_____   State_____Zip_____

PERFECT GIFTS FOR ANY OCCASION

- -

SHIP TO SHORE, INC.

10500 MT. HOLLY ROAD
CHARLOTTE, NC 28214-9347

FREE !!!

Share the taste of the Caribbean with your friends !

We will send your friends a FREE catalog. Simply mail this form or call 1-800-338-6072

Name_____   Name_____

Address_____   Address_____

City_____   City_____

State_____Zip_____   State_____Zip_____

PERFECT GIFTS FOR ANY OCCASION